FIGURE POSES FOR

FASHION ILLUSTRATORS

FIGURE POSES FOR
FASHION
ILLUSTRATORS

Sha Tahmasebi

BARRON'S

A QUARTO BOOK

First edition for North America
published in 2011 by
Barron's Educational Series, Inc.

All inquiries should be addressed to:
Barron's Educational Series, Inc.
250 Wireless Boulevard
Hauppauge, New York 11788
www.barronseduc.com

Library of Congress Control No.: 2010927823

ISBN 13: 978-1-4380-7049-0
ISBN 10: 1-4380-7049-7

QUAR.FASI

Conceived, designed, and produced by
Quarto Publishing plc
The Old Brewery
6 Blundell Street
London N7 9BH

Senior editor: Lindsay Kaubi
Art editor: Jacqueline Palmer
Designer: Anna Plucinska
Picture researcher: Sarah Bell
Copy editor: Liz Dalby
Art director: Caroline Guest

Creative director: Moira Clinch
Publisher: Paul Carslake

Color separation by Pica Digital Pte Ltd,
Singapore

Printed by 1010 Printing International
Ltd in China

9 8 7 6 5 4

Contents

Introduction	6
About this book	7
Making fashion illustrations	8
Terminology	10
Tools and materials	13

Chapter 1:

DYNAMIC FASHION FIGURES	14
Introduction to garment categories	16
Sportswear: Designer, timeless luxury	20
Sportswear: Designer, elegance	22
Sportswear: Better/bridge	24
Sportswear: Contemporary, young attitude	26
Sportswear: Sophisticated, contemporary	28
Sportswear: Junior	30
Sportswear: Missy	32
Sportswear: Women, plus-size	34
Business: Suit	36
Business: Young professional	38
Business: Professional	40
Dress: Casual	42
Dress: Day dress	44
Dress: Career dress	46
Dress: Cocktail	48
Dress: Clubwear	50
Dress: Slip dress	52
Outerwear: Contemporary/junior	54
Outerwear: Designer	56
Outerwear: Coats and capes	58

Evening wear: Prom fantasy   60
Evening wear: Bridal dress   62
Evening wear: Special occasion   64
Evening wear: Formal/semiformal   66
Swimwear and lingerie: Casual   68
Swimwear and lingerie: Luxury   70
Active sportswear: Fitness   72
Menswear: Classic   74
Menswear: Casual/sportswear   76

Chapter 2:
BASIC GARMENT BLOCKS   78

Tops: Fitted tops   80
Tops: Knits and woven   82
Tops: Using gathers   84
Sleeves: Short   86
Sleeves: All-in-one   88
Skirts: Fitted and A-line   90
Skirts: Longer and ruffled   92
Pants: Front view   94
Pants: Profile view   96
Shorts: Length and shape   98
Dresses: Short day dresses   100
Dresses: Sleeveless day dresses   102
Evening gowns: Cocktail dresses   104
Evening gowns: Long silhouette   106
Evening gowns: Profile view   108
Outerwear: Suit jackets   110
Outerwear: Casual jackets   112

Collars: Three-quarter view   114
Footwear: Boots and shoes   116
Accessories: Bags and purses   118
Men's garments: Basics   120

Chapter 3:
RENDERING TECHNIQUES   122

1: Leather   124
2: PVC   125
3: Lace   126
4: Sheer fabric   127
5: Cotton print   128
6: Animal print   129
7: Corduroy   130
8: Denim   131
9: Knitted   132
10: Stretch sports   133
11: Sequins   134
12: Stripes   135
13: Faux fur   136
14: Tweed jacket   137
15: Silk satin   138
16: Velvet   139
Digital rendering   140

Index   143
Credits   144

CD
Image files of all the line artwork featured in the book are
included on the accompanying CD at the back of the book.

Introduction

One of the most exciting and challenging roles of a designer is communicating his or her ideas clearly and convincingly to the rest of the world. This is often done visually through the drawing and rendering of a draped fashion figure. This book gives the student or illustrator the tools to create professional and detailed fashion illustrations by providing three basic variables (raw materials) and a few consistent formulas to work with. The three variables are:

- Figures in a range of fashion poses
- Basic garment blocks
- Design elements and textiles

Presented here is an array of fashion figures with different proportions and characters (most of which were developed from live models), and a palette of garment design options. The reader can select basic figure poses as the starting point and add the garment blocks to work from. These blocks can be manipulated and modified to create unique personal designs, while maintaining proportionate fashion figures—plus clothing that folds and drapes over the body realistically and artfully.

Techniques for rendering the inherent qualities of different textiles in a variety of different media are demonstrated at the end of the book by guest artists.

Sha Tahmasebi

About this book

Chapter 1: Dynamic fashion figures (pages 14–77)

This chapter is packed with nearly 150 different fashion figures in a range of poses to be used as blueprints for the development and construction of more detailed garment designs. Figures are numbered and organized into different categories, though you should not feel constrained by the categories, and may wish simply to browse through and find the perfect pose for the garment that you have in mind.

Figure category

The garments are shown in context on a scaled-down figure.

Each category features figures in a range of attitudes and poses.

Full front to three-quarter view figures.

Figures are shown dressed using garment blocks from pages 78–121, and finished using some of the rendering techniques featured on pages 122–142.

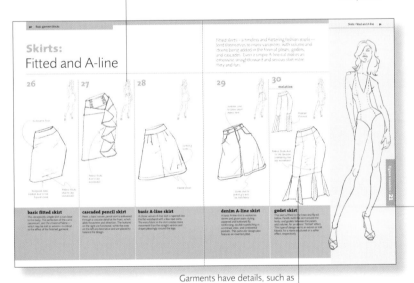

Chapter 2: Basic garment blocks (pages 78–121)

The blocks are the basic shapes of garments. You can choose from a variety of these blocks to create your own unique designs. The goal is to show how the fashion figure in Chapter 2 can be layered with basic garments, and the blocks in turn layered with the appropriate design elements.

The figure here is selected from Chapter 1. She is the template on which the clothes fit and is reproduced on the page in proportion to the garments.

The figure here is selected from Chapter 1. She is the template on which the clothes fit.

Garments have details, such as pleats, gathers, ruffles, cascades, smocking, pockets, buttons, and bows.

Chapter 3: Rendering techniques (pages 122–142)

Rendering is the process of shading, highlighting, and coloring the draped figure. When coloring a garment, there are five layers to consider: background or main color, highlights, shadows, prints, and textures. This chapter explains how to render some common textile prints and textures. Before rendering, always map the outline of each of these layers. This technique helps prevent the random and haphazard placement of colors on the drawing.

Samples of fabrics

Step by step of rendering

Making fashion illustrations

The CD

The CD supplied with this book contains all the outline artwork for you to print out and work on, or to import directly into digital art programs. The CD is compatible with both Mac and PC systems. On opening the CD, you will find numbered folders that correspond with the figure and garment numbers used in the book. The images are contained within each folder.

This book and the accompanying CD contain rights-free line-work images intended to provide reference material for the use of students, artists, and illustrators in creating their work, and as such these images may be reproduced or adapted for individual use free of charge and without permission from the copyright owner. (See copyright information on page 4 for restrictions.)

There are a multitude of ways in which you can use the illustrations in this book, whether rendering by hand, digitally, or a combination of the two. Below are step-by-step instructions for rendering a draped figure and also for how you might create a "collection." For more detailed information on rendering draped figures by hand and digitally, see pages 122–142.

Note for working by hand: The garments in the Basic garment blocks chapter are not supplied in proportion to the figures in the Dynamic fashion figures chapter, so you will need to adjust the size of one or the other, either by hand or by using a photocopier. Of course, it's always possible for you to just let your creative juices flow and simply use the garments as inspiration that you can adapt, change, and draw just as you want. For each set of garments, there is a proportional figure supplied on the page, so you can get started just by tracing.

Rendering a figure

  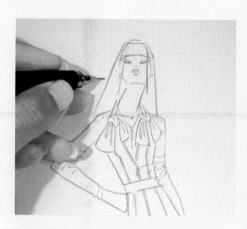

1 Choose a garment and the figure you want to drape with your chosen outfit. Here, a clubwear figure (see page 50) and cocktail dress (see page 104) have been selected. To obtain the relevant images, you could trace directly from the book, or select the appropriate image from the CD. Alternatively, you can photocopy the figure and garment that you want.

2 Place your figure on a lightbox and place a blank piece of paper on top. Keep the garment that you want to use nearby, so that you can see its details. With the lightbox on and the chosen garment in sight, practice draping your figure using the lightbox and drawing freehand. The figure will be easily visible under the blank paper. Alternatively, you could start to render the image directly in a computer program (see page 140).

3 Add your desired details, including hairstyle and accessories such as shoes (see pages 116–117), bags (see pages 118–119), jewelry, or sunglasses.

Creating a collection

1 Select a group of figures and place them on a lightbox. Here, a group from Sportswear: Designer, timeless luxury has been chosen (see pages 20–21).

2 Place a piece of paper on top of the croquis and secure with double-sided tape. Use marker paper, or thin (lightweight) watercolor paper, if you plan on rendering in watercolor.

3 With the lightbox on, you can see the figure outlines underneath. Trace around the areas of the figure that will be visible and then begin draping the figures with clothing that feels right for the pose.

4 The process of drawing should be quick and spontaneous. Your aim should be to get what's in your mind down on paper without thinking about it too much.

5 Once you have created your collection, you can always make adjustments. Below, you can see the full collection.

4 You now have a draped figure ready for rendering. If you would like to render your figure using watercolor, marker, or colored pencils (see pages 122–139); alternatively, you could continue by working digitally in a computer art program (see page 140).

5 Choose a fabric appropriate for the garment you have selected. Here, an animal-print satin and a sequin fabric have been chosen to complement the occasion the dress is designed for.

6 Scan the selected fabrics and the draped figure.

7 Render the figure using Adobe Photoshop. See pages 140–142 for step-by-step instructions on digital rendering. At right, you can see the progression of the illustration from start to finish.

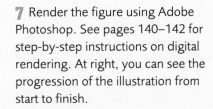

Terminology

Below is an explanation of the terminology regularly used in the book to describe the fashion figures and garments.

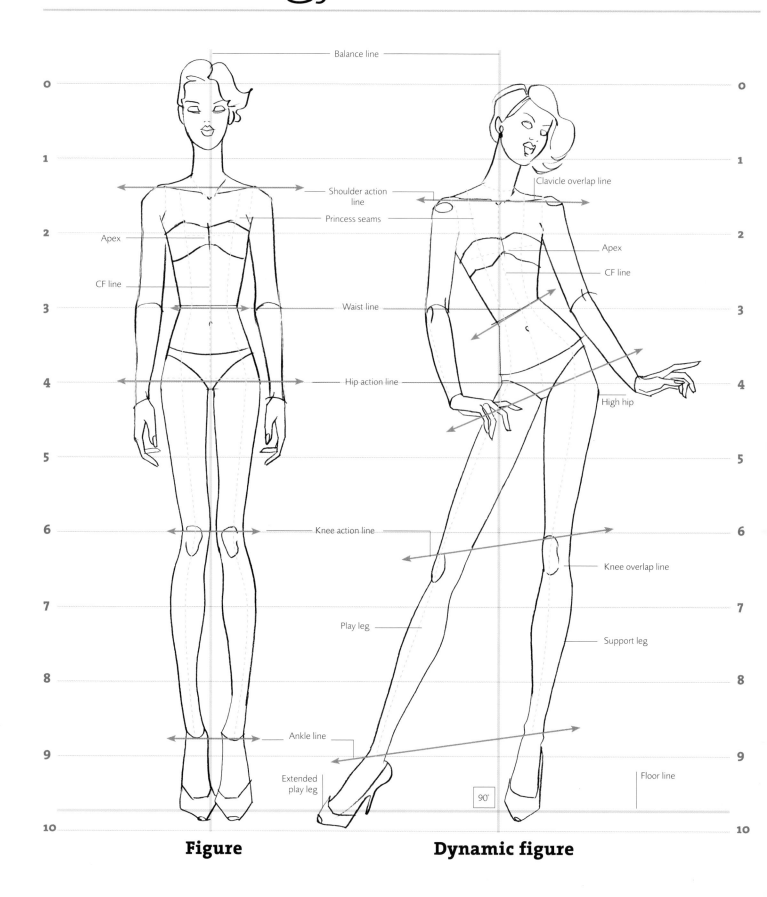

Balance line

0

1

Shoulder action line

Clavicle overlap line

Princess seams

2

Apex

Apex

CF line

CF line

3

Waist line

4

Hip action line

High hip

5

6

Knee action line

Knee overlap line

7

Play leg

Support leg

8

9

Ankle line

Floor line

Extended play leg

90°

10

Figure

Dynamic figure

Terms describing the fashion figure

Action or angle lines: These are imaginary lines created by the movement and slants of various body parts, mainly the shoulders, waist, and hips. Imaginary lines also help determine the relationship between the knees or the ankles.

Apex: The highest point of the bust.

Balance line: An imaginary line that starts from the pit of the neck and falls perpendicular to the floor. Its purpose is to help "balance" and "ground" a dynamic figure. There are guidelines that can be used to place the legs in relation to the balance line to keep the figure from looking as if it's tipping over.

Draping and sewing guideline: Imaginary lines on the body that help with the proper draping of the figure. What the balance line does for the unclothed figure, these guidelines do for the draping of a figure. They help with the proper placement and balancing of clothing on a croquis. The body has a Center-Front (CF) and a Center-Back (CB) line, and items of clothing have their corresponding centers. The seams and centers of garments should match and align with the corresponding centers and sewing guidelines on the body. They set the foundation for the placement and centering of such garment details as buttons, zippers, seams, pockets, collars, and other design elements. The main guidelines are the CF/CB lines, princess seams, armholes, neck opening, waistline, hip line, and bikini lines. The arms and the legs each have their own CF/CB lines for the proper centering and draping of garments.

Dynamic figure: A figure with movement; generally, a figure in which the hips or shoulders, or both, have movement.

High hip: The hip that's moving away from the balance line. The high hip is usually connected to the support leg.

Overlap lines: Internal nuance lines. These are subtle outlines of the structures beneath the skin, such as muscles, bones, and tendons, or lines created on the skin as a result of the turns and twists of the body. These lines act to give depth and dimension to the figure. Examples include the lines and shapes depicting the clavicle, the pit of the neck, the knees, and the scapula. Some of these shapes will be covered by the garment and some will be visible after the figure has been draped.

Play leg: The leg that's free to rotate and "play" around the body, as long as most of the weight is being held by the support leg. A trick to make figures look realistic is to draw the play leg longer than the support leg. There are always exceptions to this rule, though, as the body is capable of holding a variety of poses.

Support leg: This is the leg that supports most of the weight of the body in many common, dynamic poses. Some poses have their weight supported by both legs. The support leg shifts far away from the balance line at the hip level and comes back toward it at foot level. The importance here is that in order for the figure to look real and to look as if it's standing comfortably and not tipping off the page, the support leg comes back toward the balance line at foot or floor level.

Terms describing the draping of the fashion figure

The terms "folds," "lines," "marks," and "shadows" are used interchangeably.

Location of fabric folds and lines: Fabric folds and lines exist in two major areas of a garment:

1. Silhouette: contour of the garment:
a. Folds around the body where it bends
Example: Folds created around the waist, knees, elbows, and ankles.
b. Perspective curves
Curves of hems and necklines, armholes, cuffs, and side. Determines the overall shapes, angles, and curvatures of a garment that is worn on the body. Perspective depends on the location of the model in relation to the viewer. Example: concave, convex, or angled hemline.

2. Internal fabric folds and lines: Inside the garment. Example: folds and lines created by the movement of the body, and by the weight and drape of the fabric.

Types and causes of fabric folds and lines: Keep in mind that these factors combine to determine the overall drape of the garment on the body. For the purpose of learning and clarification, however, fabric lines and folds created on a garment are separated into the following sections:

- **Fabric:** Folds created due to the fabric itself. Determined by the inherent nature of the textile, factors such as fabric weight, fiber content, weave construction, knit, or woven.

- **Garment construction:** Fabric lines created by the design elements and construction of the garment: seams, pleats, gathers, ruffles, etc.

- **Figure's shape:** Fabric lines created due to the shape and size of the body. Lines created by the pull of gravity, causing the fabric to drape and conform around the body.

- **Figure's movement:** Fabric folds and lines created by the movement of the body itself.

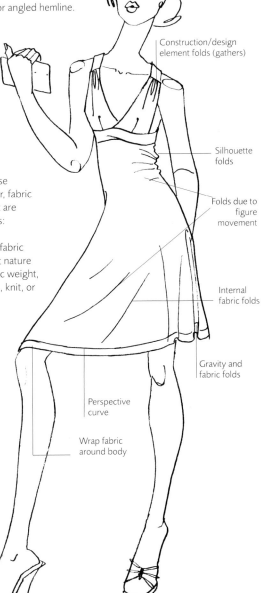

Construction/design element folds (gathers)

Silhouette folds

Folds due to figure movement

Internal fabric folds

Gravity and fabric folds

Perspective curve

Wrap fabric around body

Design element terms

Box pleats: Two pleats turned "away" from each other.

Cascade: Cascades are vertical ruffles. Fabric that is bias cut, drapes, or "cascades" vertically in folds.

Cowl: A type of design element created by draping where fabric is anchored at two points and excess is allowed to fall and loop in between. Often used as a neckline design, but also on sleeve openings, pants, and skirt sides (panier skirt).

Darts: Darts are small V-shaped tucks or folds in fabric used to create depth gradation and to conform fabric to the body. Often used in woven or stiff fabrics. Darts balance the drop or difference in width between different body parts. Example: waist darts make a rectangular piece of fabric tighter around the waist while simultaneously creating volume in the bust area.

Ease: Ease refers to the extra width in fabric that is gathered or pleated to create volume and fullness. The "ease" can be used to join a larger fabric piece to a smaller piece by distributing the fullness along the "joining" seam using gathers or pleats.

Flounce: When a decorative ruffle is attached to a hemline, it's called a flounce.

Gathers: Are created by stitching a piece of fabric and pulling the threads to create fullness in the center.

Gores: Vertical pieces of fabric sewn together to create desired shape and silhouette in a garment. A common example is a gore skirt.

Inverted pleats: Two pleats turned "toward" each other, where the edges of the two pleats meet. Note: reverse of inverted pleats can look like box pleats.

Knife pleats: Also called side or flat pleats. All pleats are folded in the same direction.

Leading edge: Where a garment opens. Fasteners are placed at stress points where the body pulls a garment open.

Openings/closures/fasteners: How clothing is secured on the body, by using buttons, zippers, lacing, Velcro, etc.

Pleats: Folds in fabric, often stitched down, to create volume, dimension, texture, and design.

Ruching: A gathered or fluted trimming made by pleating a strip of fabric so that it ruffles on both sides.

Ruffle: A piece of fabric cut circular or bias, or cut straight and gathered at the upper edge to produce ripples and folds.

Shirring: Gathers between parallel lines.

Smocking: A type of shirring with three or more rows of gathers.

Tucks: Small pleats, such as pin tucks, which are small series of parallel folds in fabric that are often secured with stitching.

Vintage smocking: Decorative needlework used to hold rows of gathers or pleats. The stitches catch alternate folds in a row in elaborate honeycomb designs. Fabric is pleated or gathered in rows, while each row of gather is connected to the next via threads alternating gathers so that triangle shapes are formed between two rows. A diamond is formed between three rows.

Yokes: Horizontal divisions in clothing. Yokes are used as control seams for incorporating gathered or pleated ease into a garment, often across the neck, shoulders, and hip areas.

Tools and materials

As in any profession, having quality tools and materials will create quality work.

Quality tools are especially important in the design world, where a presentation is essential in successfully communicating your vision and message to an audience. For some, it may involve a very sleek portfolio that is clear and direct, whereas others may have presentations that are more textured and organic in feeling. The first step in creating quality work is to ensure you have all the right tools.

General:

- Transparent ruler
- Paper scissors
- Double-sided tape
- Regular tape
- Electric eraser
- Lightbox

Papers:

- Watercolor paper: hot and cold press
- Marker paper

Drawing materials:

- Mechanical pencil and leads
- Pencils of various grades, such as HB, 2B, 2H, etc.
- Pencil sharpener

Digital tools:

- Computer
- Tablet and graphic pen

Portfolio:

- Nonzipper type suggested, with ring-binder interior that allows for pages to be changed

Media:

- Marker set: brands suggested: Copic Markers, Berol Prismacolor, Chartpak, Design Art Markers, Pantone Letraset
- Colored pencil set: 72-count suggested
- Extra white pencils
- Cold-pressed watercolor paper, cut to size to fit a portfolio of your choosing
- Brushes, such as Winsor & Newton Series 7 (7 and 2), or similar sable-hair brushes
- Paint palette with multiple wells

Watercolor paints:

Fashion illustrations must provide the viewer with an accurate depiction of color and fabric. Watercolor paint enables illustrators to match colors exactly, and depict fabric textures and weights more successfully than other, flatter mediums. From sheer chiffons to highly dense and textured yarns, watercolor has a broad range of application, and can also be used with mixed media (such as marker and colored pencil) to accurately depict designs.

Software:

The application of software in fashion illustration is virtually limitless. From creating woven patterns, printed graphics, and technical "flat" drawings in production, to concept boards used in presentations, various types of software can make the design process effective and efficient. Here are just some of the more popular applications used by illustrators.

Adobe Photoshop

A paint application (pixel-based) used primarily for creating image and photograph manipulations, composites and collages, concept boards, color palettes, select textile designs, colorways for fabric designs, basic stripe and plaid layouts, digital flats, painterly effects, texture, and rendering for digital illustration.

Adobe Illustrator

An object-oriented application (vector-based) used primarily for creating graphics, logos, font-based designs, select textile designs, drawing and rendering of illustrative flats, digital fashion illustration, and page layouts.

Drawplus

A 2-D vector graphics application with natural-looking brushes that allow you to paint with watercolors, oils, and other media, while retaining the editing capability of graphics programs. Great for producing digital fashion illustrations.

Markers

Double-sided tape

Graphic pen

Mechanical pencil

Pen

Electric eraser

Watercolor paper

Watercolor palette

Marker paper

Watercolor brush

Clockwise from the top left:
Collection by Sylvia Kwan; figure
by Nanae Takata; figure by Nanae
Takata; collection by the author.

1

Dynamic fashion figures

Different croquis inspire the creation and design of different garments and silhouettes. Sometimes you have an idea and you can search for a croquis to best show that design. But the process can also be reversed; you can start with the base croquis and be inspired to design a garment silhouette that complements the given pose.

This chapter contains a large collection of fashion figure poses. The poses are categorized based on the garments and the markets of the fashion industry. When you begin to learn draping the figure, start with poses that are relatively static and standing in the front view. This way you can focus on drawing a specific design without worrying about accurate placement of fabric folds and perspective issues. As you advance in your skills, challenge yourself with dynamic views and profile poses.

Because each section contains at least three figures, it is ideal for the creation of a collection of garments. In addition, there are a variety of body shapes and faces to choose from. Select the figure set that most inspires you and which best suits your design.

The best way to learn to draw fashion figures is to study proportion guidelines and then apply these guidelines to live model drawing. A photograph is a second-hand interpretation of a live figure. If you draw and learn exclusively from photos, your drawings and illustrations will not feel alive or accurate. Drawings based on photographs can be useful once you've mastered drawing from life. There will also come a point where drawing rules can be discarded and you can create freely, developing a unique personal style.

A quick way to know whether your draped figure is correct or not is to view your drawing in its mirror image, either by looking at it in a mirror or, if you are drawing digitally, rotating the figure on its horizontal axis. This allows your brain to see the illustration in a different light, and mistakes that might have gone unnoticed will be easily seen and corrected.

Introduction to garment categories

Women's apparel can be categorized based on two general criteria: first, the function of the garment and the occasion it is worn for (garment category), and second, the markets of the fashion industry (market category).

Garment categories are based on the function of the clothing and the occasion it is worn for. For instance, the divisions of this category include suits, bridal, and swimwear, each of which is worn for different purposes. This book covers the following garment categories: sportswear, suits and career wear, dresses, outerwear, evening wear and bridal, swimwear and lingerie, and active sportswear.

Market categories of the fashion industry are divided into different sections, depending either on price range and quality of the clothes, or are based on age, shape, and size of the wearer, with some overlap between the markets. Examples are listed below.

Sportswear (pages 20–35)

Sportswear refers to coordinated separates: tops and bottoms that are worn together. These include shirts, blouses, sweaters, and cardigans for tops, and pants, shorts, and skirts for bottoms. The term was originally used to describe clothing worn for sports, like tennis; later, for casual clothing worn for leisure activities; and now its definition has broadened to include apparel worn for a variety of occasions. Clothing for sports is now distinguished as active sportswear.

Sportswear apparel, as with most other garment categories, can be separated into different markets of the fashion industry, depending on the price range and quality of the garment, and the age, size, and body shape of the wearer. Within this section, six discrete markets have been chosen: designer, better/bridge, contemporary, (these three are based on price and quality), and junior, missy, women or plus size markets (the last three are mostly based on the wearer's age, size, and body shape).

Garment categories

- Sportswear (coordinated separates)
- Business/career/suits
- Dresses (excluding formal gowns)
- Outerwear
- Evening wear and Bridal—grouped together in the book
- Swim and Lingerie/intimate—grouped together in the book
- Active sportswear

Market categories

Market categories based on price range and quality of garments:

- Couture
- Designer
- Better/bridge
- Contemporary
- Moderate
- Budget

Market categories dependent mainly on age, size, and body shape:

- Junior (teenage and early 20s)
- Misses (35 and up)
- Petites (under 5ft. 4in./163cm)
- Women (plus size)
- Maternity

Feminine sportswear (RIGHT)
A feminine silhouette with a fitted bodice and layered skirt.

Career or formal sportswear (BELOW RIGHT)
This is a menswear-inspired designer look; the heavy tweed fabric of the pants is balanced by the lightweight satin dress top. The ruffles and sequins feminize the look.

Having a basic knowledge of various markets and customers allows you to design practical and wearable clothing. In addition, an awareness of who you're designing for allows you to choose an appropriate pose. For example, when designing sportswear for older women (misses), your choice of croquis will be different than when designing for teenagers and young women (junior).

Of course, there are no rules as far as what can be draped on a croquis, but having a good base figure to start with can make all the difference in the way garments are presented and showcased in a fashion illustration.

Markets within sportswear

The "designer" category includes the most expensive sportswear, made with impeccable craftsmanship, using the best fabrics, such as cashmeres and silks. Designer garments are sophisticated and timeless. They do not follow the trends; rather, they set them. Examples include clothing by Ralph Lauren, John Galliano, Oscar de la Renta, and Chanel. A wave of young designers has emerged relatively recently, such as Peter Som, Georgina Chapman, and Derek Lam.

When brainstorming your designs, you can choose any croquis; however, if you want to bring your idea to life and create an actual garment, you need to communicate your design concept to others and present it in a way that's relevant to your target customer. When choosing a figure to drape with a "designer" sportswear garment, imagine the woman who will eventually wear these garments: her pose and posture, the way she carries herself, her hair and makeup, accessories, and so on.

Better/bridge and contemporary designs are geared toward a wide range of customers with prices that are medium to high. Customers are usually 18 and up, and the clothes are fairly trendy. Many designers have a lower-priced diffusion line in these markets to attract a wider customer base. Examples include DKNY, RL, BCBG, and Nordstrom.

Contemporary dress
This is an asymmetrical draped dress with a rather unusual and playful hat. The dress can be worn as a contemporary day dress with sandals or appropriately accessorized for a more formal occasion.

The junior market includes trendy and fast-paced clothing with a youthful style for teenagers and women in their twenties. The prices are usually low and the fabrics are relatively cheap. Many synthetic fabrics, such as polyester and acrylic, are used to allow the production of affordable garments. Examples include Roxy, Forever 21, and Rampage. In general, the junior figure is slimmer with narrower hips and has more playful poses.

The missy market caters to the "average"-sized woman of 35 years and older. The clothes are comfortable and practical for everyday wear. They are about functionality rather than trend. Examples include Talbot and Anne Taylor. Choosing a croquis with the right body proportions and appropriate pose will aid in the presentation of your design ideas.

Women—this is the market that caters to plus-size women (U.S. sizes 16 and upward). Brands like Liz Claiborne and Chadwicks offer clothing for this market. Again, think of the croquis and poses that would work for a plus-size figure. The figures presented in this book represent an idealized larger woman.

Business (pages 36–41)

Career wear is clothing worn for business, and includes suits, dresses, and more formal sportswear. These garments are generally more tailored, and contain design elements that add a sense of professionalism to the outfit, such as collars, cuffs, lining, and design seams.

Dresses (pages 42–53)

A dress is the ultimate feminine garment. Designs and silhouettes are endless: short, medium, or long hemlines, with or without sleeves, fitted or loose, high or low waistline. Some popular styles are the maxidress, with a long silhouette, Asian-influenced kimono dresses with wide sleeves, empire-waist dresses with a high waistline, wrap dresses as popularized by Diane von Furstenberg in the 1970s, and shirt dresses that resemble a collared shirt but are long enough to be worn as a dress. Dresses are subcategorized based on the occasion they're worn for; those covered in this book are sun/casual dresses, work/ career dresses, cocktail and clubwear, and slip and lounge dresses. Evening gowns fall into their own category.

Outerwear (pages 54–59)

Jackets, coats, and capes are worn over other garments to provide protection against the weather and elements of nature. Jackets are often hip length or shorter. Coats are longer than jackets, and capes are sleeveless outerwear that wrap around the body and can have slits acting as armholes.

Evening/special occasion dress
This is a strapless special occasion dress with a feathered skirt. A dress like this is hand crafted and used as a showcase piece for fashion runways, rather than as a marketable and saleable garment.

Evening wear (pages 60–67)

Evening gowns are usually long in silhouette and worn for formal occasions, such as weddings, soirées, and ceremonial functions. For the high-end spectrum, embellished fabrics with sequins and hand beading, silk georgettes, chiffons, and satins are used. Because they are worn for special events, many are handmade and not mass-produced.

Swimwear and lingerie (pages 68–71)

These two groups are placed together because they share some basic garment silhouettes, yet they belong to distinct garment categories. Each has gone through drastic evolutionary changes over time, from the full body bathing dresses of the early 20th century to the modern skin-revealing designs of the new millennium. The use of stretch fibers like spandex revolutionized body hugging garments and resulted in more comfortable and practical swimwear and lingerie.

Active sportswear (pages 72–73)

Apparel worn for sports like tennis, snowboarding, and running. Here, fiber and textile innovations play an important role; fabrics with properties that enable easier body movements, transfer heat, and are moisture-resistant greatly enhance the durability and function of these garments.

Menswear (pages 74–77)

Men's apparel takes up a smaller share of the fashion industry, with steady expansion in recent years. Menswear can be formal, consisting of suits and collared shirts, or casual clothing worn for day-to-day activities, as well as undergarments, sleepwear, and clothing for swim and sports.

Casual dress
A casual summer dress with a tropical-style border print design and embellished stripes. The short length and floral print makes this design appropriate for a younger customer base.

Sportswear:
Designer, timeless luxury

1

2

3

full front view

This figure has a relaxed pose, with the upper body twisting toward the viewer. The upper and lower torso princess lines aid in the communication of this subtle twist. The figure's right hand could be used to show off a purse design. The pose would work for an off-the-shoulder top over a pair of Capri pants.

full front view, hands on waist

This model is hugging her waist, an ideal pose to display garments fitted at the waist and upper hip. The model's left leg is bent and her knee is closer to the viewer, creating an angled "knee line." Lightly shade the right leg shin to show this depth. A full front view is a practical way of showcasing a design without the distraction of body movements. It would be a good pose for a collared blouse design with a fitted skirt.

three-quarter front view

The right leg is the supporting leg, while the play leg recedes and appears shorter. By lightly shading the model's left calf, you can emphasize this spatial difference. (Another way to depict this would be to draw the foot closer to you slightly larger.) The hips and shoulders have some movement, and this can be used to add additional folds and dimensions to the garments. This would be a great pose for a batwing top and a pair of classic pants.

This collection of figures was developed for designer sportswear day wear. Designer clothing is expensive and made to last. To remain relevant for years, the styles cannot follow trends; rather, they must set them. The figures here parallel that concept; poses are simple, yet exude confidence without being subject to fashion illustration trends.

Bubble-sleeve top and red miniskirt

This figure has been draped and rendered using Copic markers on Canson marker paper.

The bold solid colors of the hair and the skirt are balanced with the soft beige of the top. The hair color is kept solid with a bit of the white of the paper peeking through for light.

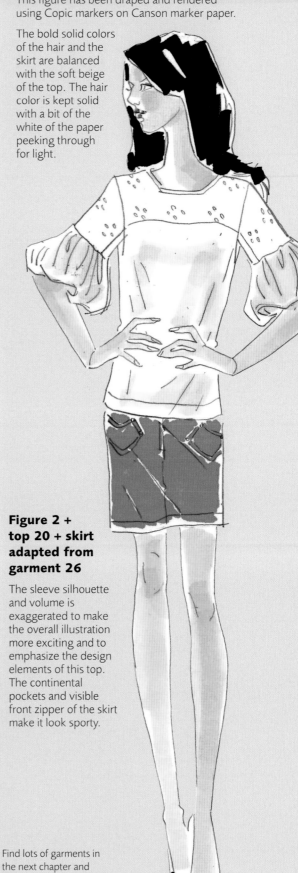

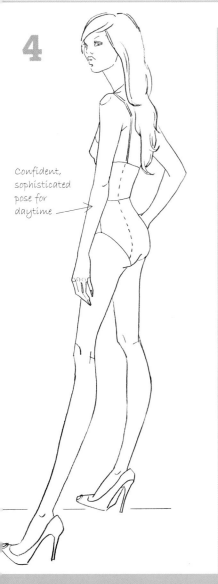

4

Confident, sophisticated pose for daytime

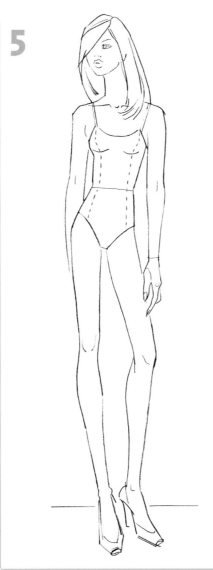

5

three-quarter back view

The model's extended leg is closer to the viewer and appears longer than the right leg. Both legs support her weight. Note the model's right foot: you can see partially under the plane of the shoe; this small detail adds a nice touch to the overall look of the pose. This figure is relaxed and would be ideal for sportswear pieces that have back and profile details.

full front view, relaxed

This simple pose is perfect for depicting the front details of a garment. The right hand is placed behind the hip to prevent obstruction of garments. Lightly shade the model's left calf to show the "bend" in the knee. The hips and shoulders are fairly straight and static—ideal for showing garments without the hindrance of body movement. It would be great for an A-line skirt design with a puff-sleeved top.

Figure 2 + top 20 + skirt adapted from garment 26

The sleeve silhouette and volume is exaggerated to make the overall illustration more exciting and to emphasize the design elements of this top. The continental pockets and visible front zipper of the skirt make it look sporty.

Find lots of garments in the next chapter and adjust them to fit your chosen figure pose.

Sportswear:
Designer, elegance

6

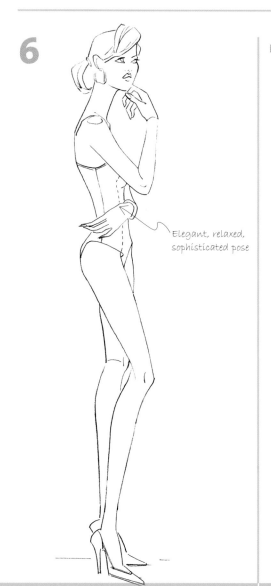

Elegant, relaxed, sophisticated pose

7

8

profile view

This profile figure is relaxed yet sophisticated. It's a classic pose that can be used to show garment details not otherwise visible in a front view. Drawing the side seams of garments adds a realistic touch to a fashion illustration. When designing a collection of garments, it's a good idea to show a profile view along with the front views.

full front view, subtle hip movement

The model's left leg is forward and closer to the viewer, so it appears longer than her right leg. To clearly depict this depth difference, lightly shade the model's right calf. The lifted arm could hold a purse at the elbow to showcase accessories.

full back view

Here the hair is purposely lifted up to enhance the attention given to the garment draped over this figure. The hips are angled to the right, yet both legs support the weight of the body. Note the overlap lines of the elbow, and back-of-the knee tendons, and their use in depicting the back view of the figure.

The figures in this group have been created for high-end designer sportswear clothing. The poses are comfortable and exude elegance and confidence. The overall play of hands adds a feminine touch to the group. The clothing designed for these figures will be of high-quality fabrics and impeccable craftsmanship.

Layered dress-coat over pants

This figure has been rendered using Adobe Photoshop.

The layered dress coat is made of gingham fabric with a leather collar and trimmings. A dress worn over pants creates a sportier look. The white of the paper is left untouched to act as the shine and highlight, as well as to create separation between the layers of the skirt piece.

Figure 7 + dress 73

The volume of the hair is exaggerated for a sophisticated up-do.

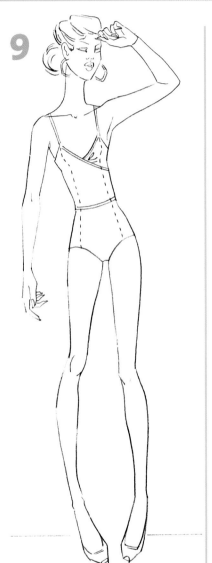

9

10

full front view

Here, both legs support the weight of the pose. Both hands are away from the body to allow full view of the garments. The left hand may be used to show off hat designs. Note the use of the clavicle and underarm overlap line in the lifted arm to add depth. Because of the static nature of this pose and clear full front view, garment designs will remain the main focus.

full front view, relaxed

The arm lifted over the head signals confidence. Note the use of shoulder overlap lines. The model's right leg is bent and is closer to the viewer. This creates an angled "knee line" and one leg that appears longer than the other. To simplify the drawing of hands, draw each finger as a simple shape, as shown here, with the model's left hand on her hip.

Sportswear:
Better/bridge

11

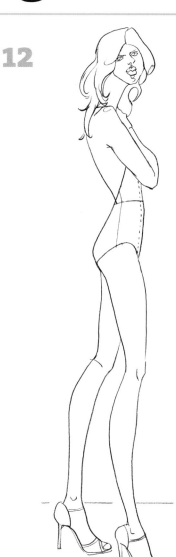

12

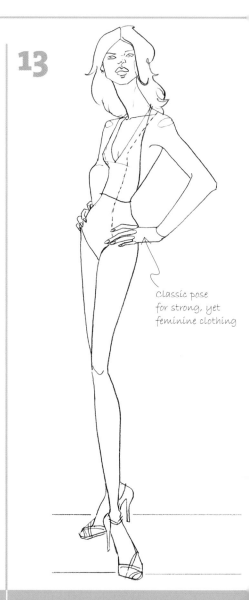

13

Classic pose for strong, yet feminine clothing

three-quarter front view

A strong stance with a confident attitude. This is a classic fashion pose seen over decades of fashion history, especially in the 1950s and 1960s. The model places one foot in front of the other for elegance. The shoulders are tilted back and the hip is fairly straight. This would be a good pose for a long, fitted, high-waist skirt with a halter top.

profile view

A simple and relaxed profile pose with one leg in front of the other. The profile also functions to further slim the fashion figure so that garments with fullness and volume or a larger silhouette in general still look flattering. This would work for a casual strapless top, and a circle or pleated skirt with lots of volume. It would also be good for simultaneously showing pants' inseam and outseam details. Always show the side seam when draping a profile figure; it enhances the realistic feel.

three-quarter front view, with attitude

This woman has command of her surroundings, yet the placement of one foot in front of the other creates a feminine stance. This pose is similar to the first, yet the hips are tilted away from the viewer and less of the upper body is visible. The left princess seam is visible and the right disappears from view. It would be great for a long, bishop-sleeved knit top and a fitted skirt or a pair of wide-leg denims.

"Better/bridge" and contemporary markets cater to a wide array of customers. The garments in these categories are medium- to high-quality for women of all ages. This is a group of classic fashion poses. The figures exude confidence and intelligence, and are ideal for more formal sportswear.

Peasant top with bishop sleeves

This figure has been draped and rendered using Copic markers on Canson marker paper.

This illustration boldly displays a large gingham print, while the rendering of the skin and hair are kept light, and the skirt and shoes are devoid of color. The white of the paper is allowed to show through the skin and hair rendering for highlights.

Figure 13 + top 10 + skirt adapted from garment 30

The shapes of both the top and the skirt have been exaggerated, the sleeve volume is increased while the skirt hem has been narrowed to an unrealistic width. This exaggeration creates a more harmonious silhouette. You can show your garments in their best view while staying true to the design.

profile view, twisted

Most of the body's weight is supported on the left leg. The left princess seam is visible and may be used for the correct placement of pockets and seams when draping the figure. Because the model has both arms lifted, you can use that to draw attention to sleeve silhouettes. This would be excellent for a short kimono or cape-sleeved top with deep armholes, worn with wide-leg or sailor pants.

back view, hip tilted

The model is standing with her hips tilted to the left and supporting her weight on the corresponding leg. Nuance lines on her back add depth to the figure.

Sportswear:
Contemporary, young attitude

16

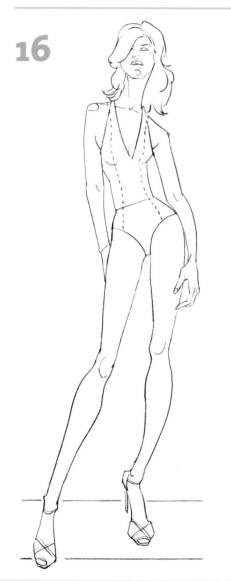

17

Fun and flirty pose for trendy pieces

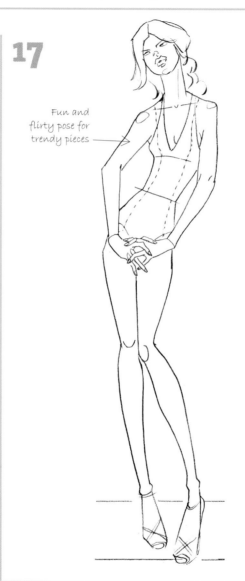

18

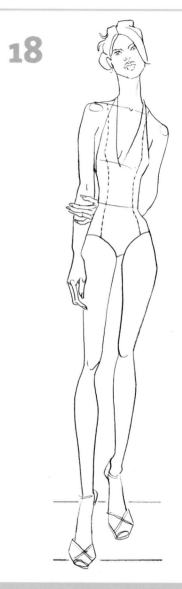

front view, dynamic

This is a popular fashion illustration pose, with the hip slanted to the left and the shoulders angled in the opposite direction. Where the low shoulder meets the high hip (on the left side of the model), garments will take on more fabric folds and lines. Note how the supporting leg comes back toward the center front line of the body. The play leg is free to move and is drawn longer for balance. It would work for a pair of shorts and a draped, loose, one-shoulder top.

front view, hands clasped

The tilted head creates a fun and youthful pose. The hip movement is exaggerated and the shoulders are angled. The model's right leg supports most of the body weight: it's far from the balance line at hip level, moving back toward the balance line at foot level. That's why this figure can stand on the page without appearing as if it's tipping over, despite its exaggerated hip and shoulder movements. The hands may be used to draw attention to garment detailing below hip level. It would be good for a loose-fitting, cowl-neck top with skinny pants.

front view, arm behind

The tilted head suggests a youthful and curious disposition. The figure is standing fairly straight; the dynamics come from the right leg extending forward toward the viewer. Because this leg is closer to the viewer, it is drawn longer. To communicate this dynamic more clearly, lightly shade the leg that's farther away. Note how the left foot aligns with the pit of the neck. This would be great for a top with raglan sleeves and a denim miniskirt.

These figures were created to clearly show the full front details of sportswear garments. They have lots of hip and shoulder movement as a group. The poses are fun and playful, and are appropriate for a youthful and trendy contemporary collection.

Cape-sleeve top and fitted denim

This figure has been draped and rendered using Copic and Prismacolor markers on the back side of Canson marker paper.

Different shades of gray are used for the garments, along with a lighter hair color to keep the illustration relatively monochromatic. To unify the picture, the blue color moves around the figure: on the neckline, bracelets, purse, and the heels of the shoes. The twill weave of the denim is represented by softly drawn diagonal lines.

Figure 16 + top 25 + pants 37

A few sparkles are added to the jeweled top and the bracelets for shine and highlight.

19

20

three-quarter view, arm lifted

This figure is slightly turned away from the viewer, creating a three-quarter view of the pose. The lifted arm allows for viewing the garment's armhole shape and seams. Because the legs cross one another, a very slim silhouette is created toward the bottom of the pose. It would work for a dolman-sleeved tunic with fitted Capri pants.

front view, head tilted

A youthful pose with a tilted head. The hands add to the playful feel—use them to enhance your designs. The right leg is extended forward and appears longer; to better show this depth, lightly shade the leg that's farther away from the viewer. This would be great for a blouse with bodice pin-tucking and ruffled cap sleeves, worn with a prairie skirt.

Sportswear:
Sophisticated, contemporary

21

22

23

three-quarter front view, dynamic

This figure has both horizontal and vertical dynamics. The hips and shoulders have opposing action lines for horizontal movement and the upper torso is bent toward the pelvis, creating vertical motion. The model's right leg is the play leg and is drawn longer than the support leg because of its proximity to the viewer.

front view, dynamic

An elegant and slim pose. Most of the figure's weight is supported by the right leg, and the play leg crosses over to the front. The shoulders and hips have opposing action lines, creating movement in the pose. The head is tilted to balance the dynamics of the legs.

three-quarter sitting pose

The arms support the upper body on the seat. Because this is a sitting pose, the figure is further slimmed and a different silhouette is created relative to the full front pose. The outline of the bust becomes visible on one side as the figure turns away from the view. Study the neck and shoulder area, and note the clavicle and neck overlap lines adding depth to the figure. For a soft and feminine look, keep your overlap lines subtle after the figure has been draped with garments.

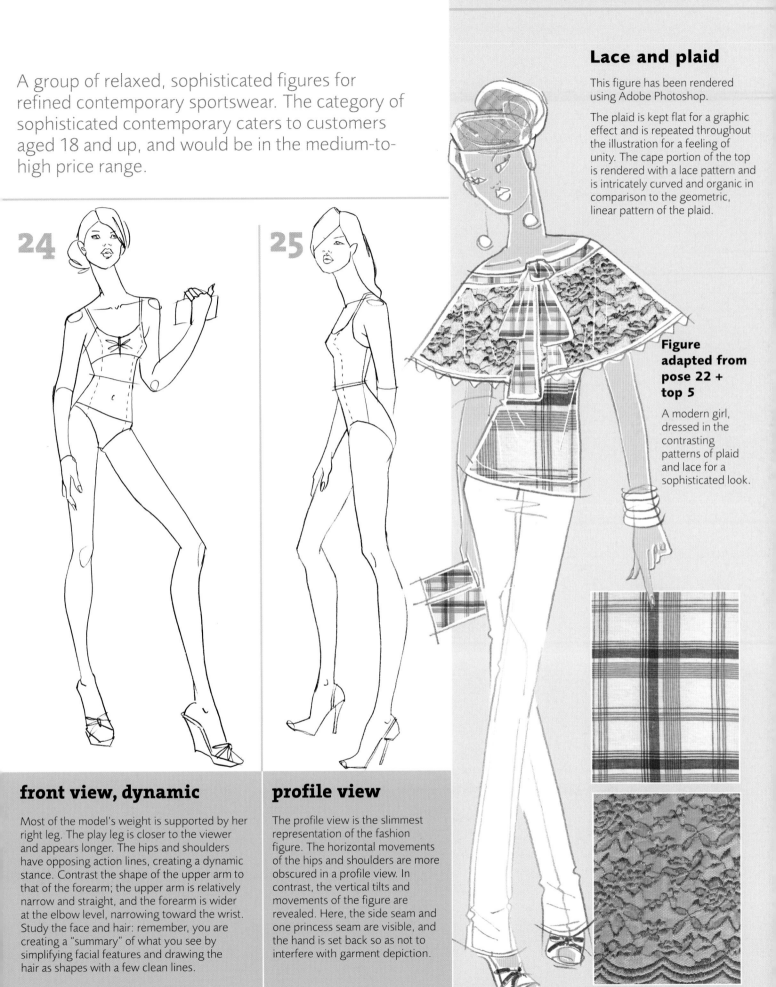

A group of relaxed, sophisticated figures for refined contemporary sportswear. The category of sophisticated contemporary caters to customers aged 18 and up, and would be in the medium-to-high price range.

24

25

Lace and plaid

This figure has been rendered using Adobe Photoshop.

The plaid is kept flat for a graphic effect and is repeated throughout the illustration for a feeling of unity. The cape portion of the top is rendered with a lace pattern and is intricately curved and organic in comparison to the geometric, linear pattern of the plaid.

Figure adapted from pose 22 + top 5

A modern girl, dressed in the contrasting patterns of plaid and lace for a sophisticated look.

front view, dynamic

Most of the model's weight is supported by her right leg. The play leg is closer to the viewer and appears longer. The hips and shoulders have opposing action lines, creating a dynamic stance. Contrast the shape of the upper arm to that of the forearm; the upper arm is relatively narrow and straight, and the forearm is wider at the elbow level, narrowing toward the wrist. Study the face and hair: remember, you are creating a "summary" of what you see by simplifying facial features and drawing the hair as shapes with a few clean lines.

profile view

The profile view is the slimmest representation of the fashion figure. The horizontal movements of the hips and shoulders are more obscured in a profile view. In contrast, the vertical tilts and movements of the figure are revealed. Here, the side seam and one princess seam are visible, and the hand is set back so as not to interfere with garment depiction.

Sportswear:
Junior

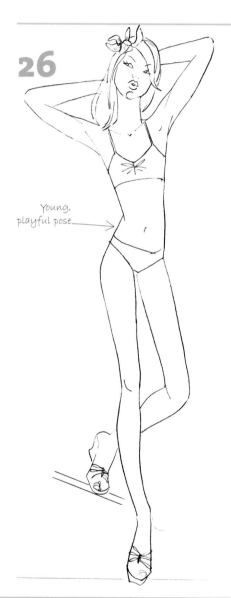

26

Young, playful pose

27

28

front view, dynamic

A free and fun pose with movement in both the arms and the legs. The left leg recedes, creating foreshortening of the lower leg. To show depth, lightly shade the calf. The right leg supports most of the weight of the body, and the model's right foot is aligned with the balance line. Drawing the arms in the lifted position can be challenging. Play with the shape and angles of the clavicle and underarm overlap lines to accurately depict them.

front view, hand gestures

There is a youthful attitude to this pose, with one hand on the waist. The other may be used to show off accessories, such as rings and bracelets, to enhance your designs. The right leg is bent at the knee and recedes; by lightly shading below the knee, you can better communicate this foreshortening. Most of the weight is supported on the left leg.

three-quarter view, dynamic

This figure is turned away from the viewer, creating a three-quarter view, and you can see the outline of the bust on one side. The right leg is placed on a platform and it may be used to show garments' silhouettes, such as the fullness of a flared dirndl skirt, or design elements, such as hem detailing of pants.

These figures were created for rapid, trendy, and disposable fashion. The poses are playful with a bit of attitude. The hips are narrower than the shoulders, and in general there are less exaggerated curvatures to the body. There are lots of hand gestures, which can be used to complement your designs and accessories.

Kimono sleeve top and denim shorts

This figure has been draped and rendered using Copic markers on marker paper.

The rib knitting on the top's neckline and waistband is indicated with subtle marker lines. Fabric folds show through the garment to communicate the drape of the top.

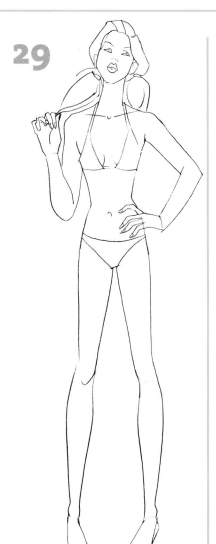

29

30

Figure 26 + top adapted from garment 22 + shorts 50

For this junior market sportswear outfit, a simple monotone rendering technique has been used throughout the figure, with no shading.

full front view

A fairly static stance, where the tilt in the head and the arms creates the dynamics of the pose. Because of the straight angles of the shoulders, hips, and knees, this is a simple figure to drape. Here, the focus can be on your designs, rather than worrying about correctly draping garments on a figure.

front view, crossed arms

In general, you will want to use poses with unobstructed views of the garments. However, there are times when you may want to draw attention to specific areas of the design or outfit. Here, the attention can be diverted to the neckline and the legs. The tilted head suggests a youthful attitude.

Sportswear:
Missy

31

32

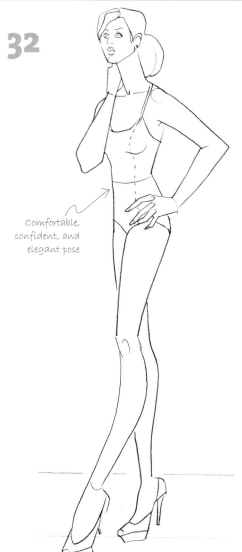

Comfortable, confident, and elegant pose

33

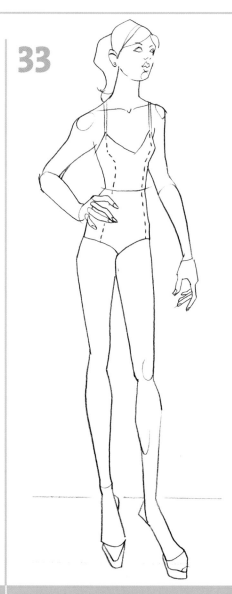

three-quarter front view

Both hands are positioned at the waist and both legs support the body equally. The left arm is foreshortened, and the left hand is only partially visible. To simplify the drawing of hands, draw each finger individually as seen here. Looking at the face, note dyne diagonal angle of the imaginary eye level and the lip lines.

three-quarter front view, dynamic

The extended left leg adds elegance and length to the body. The left arm may remain on the hip or may be placed inside a garment's pocket. The left princess seam is visible and could be used for the placement of design elements and seams. Note the subtle overlap line under the figure's left arm.

full front view

A comfortable and relaxed pose with a subtle hip movement. The right leg supports most of the body's weight. Note the extension of the play leg; this lengthening creates a more balanced figure on the page. The model's left arm moves back and away from the viewer and is foreshortened.

This market caters to the "average"-sized (idealized) woman of 35 years and up. These are poses intended for comfortable and practical everyday wear that are more about functionality than trend. The poses are not overly exaggerated in hip and shoulder movements, and exude comfort and ease.

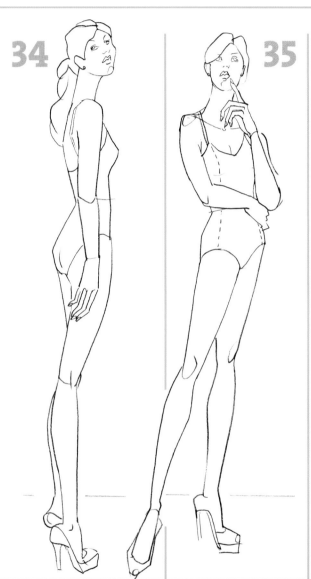
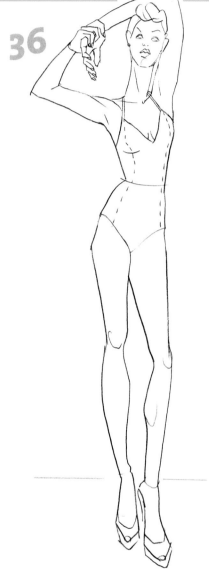
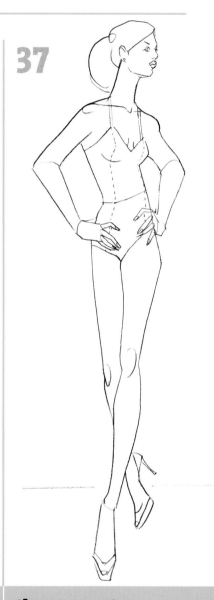

three-quarter back view

The head is lifted up, elongating the neck for an elegant and confident look. Note the use of overlap lines at the back of the knee and the ankle bone: these add depth and dimension as well as communicating which angle the body is at. Studying the three-quarter face, you can see that the left eye is partially hidden by the bridge of the nose.

three-quarter front view

A pensive and intelligent pose. The hip is slanted to the left and, correspondingly, most of the body's weight is supported on the left leg. The right arm covers the waist, diverting attention away from it.

front view, arms lifted

A comfortable pose with an easy stance. The hip sways to the right and the play leg is extended forward. Drawing the play leg longer creates a "balanced" figure. Study the overlap lines under the arm and the shoulder area, and how they are used to create depth and realism where the arms are lifted up. A quick and sure way to show different moods in your models is to play with the eyebrows. Experiment with their angles and position.

three-quarter view, twisted

The upper body twists away from the viewer, while the lower half rotates in the opposite direction. You can see this shift in movement by looking at the princess seams. The left arm is foreshortened and so appears shorter than the right arm. The play leg is bent back and is drawn shorter than the support leg. You can show depth by shading the small portion of the play leg visible below the knee.

Sportswear:
Women, plus-size

38

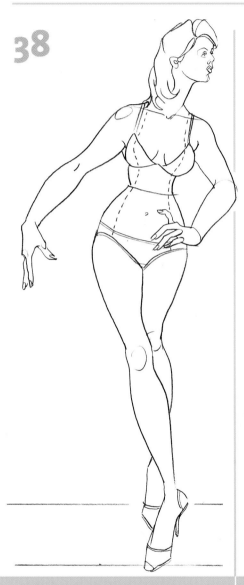

39

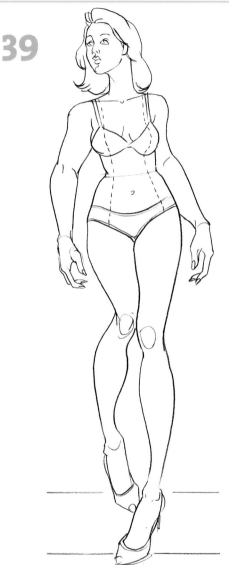

40

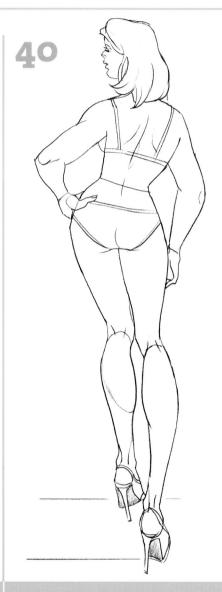

front view, dynamic

The hip is slanted to the right, and its corresponding leg comes forward. Because of the unusual stance, both legs merge at the balance line to ground the figure. To simplify the drawing of hands, pay attention to each finger and draw them individually, while elongating them all equally. The right arm is lifted up and away from the body, good for draping with bishop- or bell-sleeved tops. The legs' merging creates a narrow silhouette toward the ankles, great for slim pants or fitted skirts.

front view, walking

This pose has lots of movement, and the draped figure should complement this dynamic. The figure's left foot is closer to the viewer and appears longer. You can also draw the closer foot slightly larger to communicate the spatial difference between the feet. Notice how the clavicle, underarm, elbow, and wrist overlap lines create depth. Hands can be challenging, so memorize a few common hand shapes and reproduce them on similar poses.

full back view

The left hand on the hip is a sign of confident attitude. There is a subtle twist in the upper torso, and by playing with the dynamics of the scapula overlap lines you can depict this movement. Note the center back line on the figure curving along and following the spine. Other overlap lines that help in depiction of the back view are the elbow, hip, bottom, and back knee and ankle tendons. The model's right leg and foot are closer to the viewer and hence appear longer than the left.

These poses were created for plus-sizes, and represent an idealized version of a larger woman. As a group, the figures are highly dynamic, with lots of emotions and movements. When creating a collection, it's important to keep the figures' body proportions and heights consistent.

41

42

A dynamic, energized, larger woman

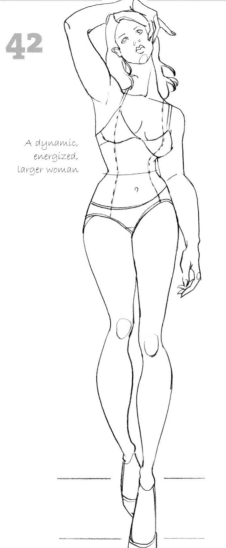

43

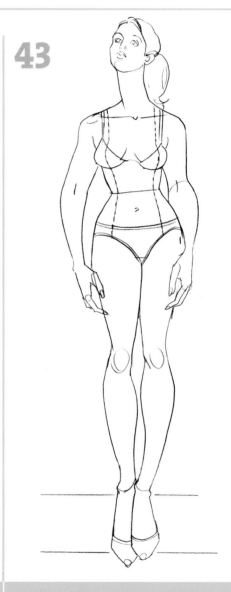

profile view

The right clavicle is visible and is foreshortened. The right princess seam is also visible, which helps with the placement of seams and design elements such as pockets and buttons. Study the face in profile: note the angle that's created, going from the tip of the nose to the chin. Be careful not to protrude the chin forward, or your figure will take on more masculine features.

front view, arm lifted

The shoulders are angled and the clavicle follows this shift. The right arm lifted above the head gives this pose a more casual feel. Note how the underarm and shoulder muscle overlap lines add depth and dimension to the lifted arm area. The model's left leg is closer to the viewer and so is drawn longer. The corresponding foot is drawn slightly larger to convey this depth difference.

full front view, static

This figure can act as a "hanger" for a plus-size model to simply depict garments in their front view. There are no movements, and in many instances a fully static pose is the most practical way of depicting clothes and their details. The face has emotion and attitude to bring life to this pose. Study the princess seams, the waistline, arm lengths, and other proportions that are the blueprint for the creation of the more dynamic figures in this group.

Business:
Suit

profile view

A slim and narrow silhouette, with one arm resting on the hip. The face is three-quarter view, with the outline of the cheek visible on one side. This would be good for depicting side pocket and sleeve cuff detailing: try a belted jacket with a princess-seam pocket worn over a dress shirt and a fitted skirt with side slits.

full front view

The hips and shoulders are fairly static; the play leg turns inward toward the center front line. The model's left arm is foreshortened. The left hand is resting on the low hip and can be placed inside garment pockets. This would be great for a fitted tuxedo vest and sailor pants, with a jacket held on the model's right hand. Accessorize with oversized chain necklaces.

front view, dynamic

This model has both horizontal and vertical movements, with the upper torso leaning toward the viewer. The hips are tilted back and the pelvis appears shorter. The support leg is behind the play leg. Note the knee and ankle action lines and how they depict depth. The face slants to the left to balance the shift of the upper torso. The hands may be used to highlight pocket design and placement. This would work for a notched-collar, single-breasted jacket with three-quarter length sleeves and a waist peplum, worn with a pleated skirt.

"Suit" refers to a two- or three-piece garment consisting of a jacket, a skirt or a pair of pants, and a vest of matching fabric. What's common to suits is their tailoring and structured foundation for support and fit. They usually consist of layers of lining and interfacings for reinforcement of shape and fit.

47

48

The hand is used to showcase the hat

Tailored jacket

This figure has been draped and rendered using Adobe Photoshop.

The spotted fabric was created in Photoshop and dropped into the jacket; attention was given to the direction of the pattern. The skin tone and blocked color were generated using a variety of Photoshop textured brushes. Using the opacity tool enables you to build on the color, creating a softer feel. A mock-croc texture was collaged into the accessories to give more dimension and depth.

Figure 45 + tailored jacket adapted from garment 77

A young, fun tailored look for day wear. Shortening the body and sleeve of the jacket has altered its style, creating a younger look and feel.

full front view, static

Both legs support the figure's weight, with the right leg extending forward and drawn longer than the other. Note the knee and ankle action lines and how they show that the legs are on different planes. The face is in three-quarter view, with one eye farther away from the viewer, appearing smaller. This pose would be good for a hip-length jacket with princess seams, welt pockets, and a deep collar roll, worn with slim pants cuffed at the hem.

front view, leaning back

The left princess seam is fully visible while the right seam outlines the torso. Note how the clavicle, neck, and underarm nuance lines add depth. Keep internal lines light and clean, and know the purpose of each. This would work for a loose-fitting, trapeze-shaped vest with flap pockets, worn over a collared blouse. A long, straight-line skirt with front pleating would give this pose a 1930s silhouette. Accessorize with a scarf around the neck and a briefcase in the left hand.

Business:
Young professional

49

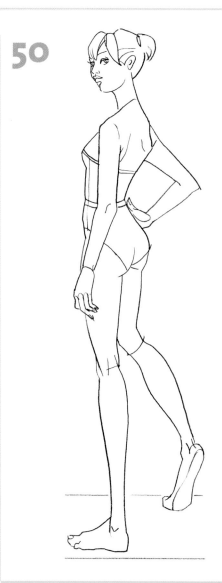

50

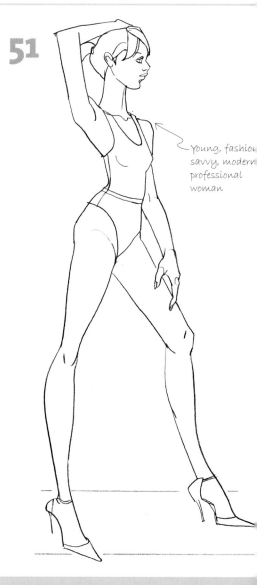

51

Young, fashion savvy, modern professional woman

profile view

An easy and fairly casual pose, good for showing a garment's silhouette and drape. Most of the weight is supported on the model's left leg. Study the face and neck: to create an elegant look, bring the neckline back away from the chin. Note the overlap lines on the neck, elbow, and knee, adding depth to the figure. This pose would be great for a short-sleeved, turtleneck sweater with a long, trapezoid silhouette and extra-wide hem, worn over cigarette pants.

three-quarter back view

This pose exudes a mixture of confidence and coyness to show off back detailing. The left hand position allows for the depiction of cuff detailing not otherwise visible in a front view. Note the model's scapula and the back-of-the-knee overlap lines, which clarify the angles of the pose and add depth to the drawing. This would suit a yoke-collared blouse top with back gathers, worn over a pair of pants with interesting back pockets.

three-quarter front view, arm lifted

This model's legs are far apart—a strong, masculine stance softened by the arm resting on the head. Note the diagonal angle from the tip of the nose to the bottom of the chin. In a profile view, this slope helps to feminize faces. Study the area around the neck and underarm. The clavicle and shoulder overlap lines help to define this area. Be careful not to crowd your figure with unnecessary lines; keep these marks clean and few. This would be a good pose for a cowl-armhole top over a pair of wide-leg pants.

This section focuses on more formal sportswear appropriate for career and business. The figures represent a young, professional, fashion-conscious woman. Career clothing is generally structured and tailored; therefore, the main goal of these poses is to clearly show construction details. These figures as a group are good for contemporary work clothes.

52

53

54

three-quarter front view, walking

This pose is elegant and feminine. The model's play leg is stretched forward and drawn longer than the support leg. Note the angles of the shoulder and the hip. The model's right foot aligns with the pit of the neck (the start of the balance line). It would be great for a buttoned-down collar blouse with puff sleeves and a mid-calf skirt with waist gathers.

three-quarter front view, assertive

A strong, intelligent pose. Most of the weight is supported on the model's left leg, with the right leg farther away, hence appearing shorter. When drawing the hands, start with simple geometric shapes, and define and contour the fingers once the basic shape is correctly placed on paper. This pose would work for a long, fitted blazer worn with a pair of pants fitted through the thighs and flaring slightly toward the hem.

profile view, shoulders back

Study the relationship between the knees and note the diagonal angle that's created connecting them: this imaginary line helps with the drawing of the figure. In a profile pose, the back of the hand can be fully visible, so memorize a good, common hand pose to utilize when drawing from memory. This would be a good pose for a V-neck blouse with elbow-length bell sleeves and a fitted, knee-length skirt with a side slit.

Business:
Professional

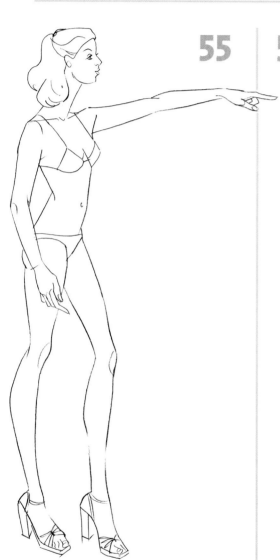

55

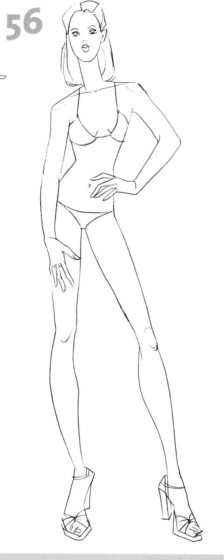

56

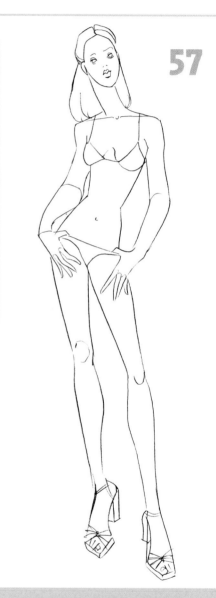

57

three-quarter view

A strong, commanding pose. Most of the attention is focused on the extended arm, so use it to showcase special sleeve designs. Note the overlap lines at the clavicle, shoulder, underarm, elbow, waist, and knee, all helping to define angles and add depth to this figure. It would work for a fitted blazer worn over a bishop-sleeved V-neck blouse with straight-leg pants or a pleated skirt. Use the right hand to hold a business bag or small luggage.

full front view

A strong, confident pose, with the hand on the waist. The legs are relatively far apart and the shoulders' slant is exaggerated. The model's left hand on the waist can be studied and used for many full front view poses. This pose would be good for an oversized knit cardigan with ribbed boat neckline and wide sleeve opening, worn over a buttoned-down collar blouse. A pair of high-waist fitted pants with center front piping would complement this pose.

full front view, dynamic

A strong pose with attitude. Note the angles of the hip and shoulder lines. The support foot aligns with the pit of the neck, and the play leg extends forward and is drawn longer. The right shoulder is tilted back, creating foreshortening o the arm. The hands can be placed inside pockets to showcase their designs or may rest on a low-waist pair of pants. This would be great with a fitted vest worn over a cropped bishop-sleeved knit top and a low-rise pair of pants with a wide cuff. Add a neck scarf to accessorize this pose.

Career sportswear for an established, professional woman. The figures in this group show a woman in control. Sportswear pieces designed for a more professional career look will feature details such as princess seams, collars, cuffs, and linings that add structure and formality to a look.

Vest, shirt, and princess-seam skirt

This figure has been rendered using Adobe Photoshop and draped using Illustrator.

Each garment piece has its own layer, so you can manipulate and modify them individually to create different versions of your illustration. The vest, skirt, and blouse textiles, and the ostrich leather texture can all be modified.

58

59

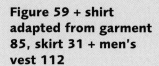

Figure 59 + shirt adapted from garment 85, skirt 31 + men's vest 112

A combination of fabrics is used for textural variety. The shirt is layered with a vest to add dimension.

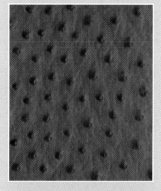

three-quarter view, arm lifted

This is a softer, more relaxed pose. The upper torso is tilted upright for a confident posture. Most of the body's weight is supported on the model's left leg, with the play leg crossed over to create a slim silhouette toward the feet. This pose would be good for a halter-style fitted vest with princess seams and wide-leg pants.

full front view, expressive

Here, the high hip is slanted to the left and connected to the support leg. The play leg is bent and comes closer to the viewer, hence is drawn longer. Utilize the lifted arm to showcase unique design elements of the garment. This pose would be good for a waist-length blazer with wide epaulettes and cuff detailing, worn over a buttoned-down collar blouse and a low-rise, relaxed-fitting skirt, hemmed right at the knee.

Dress:
Casual

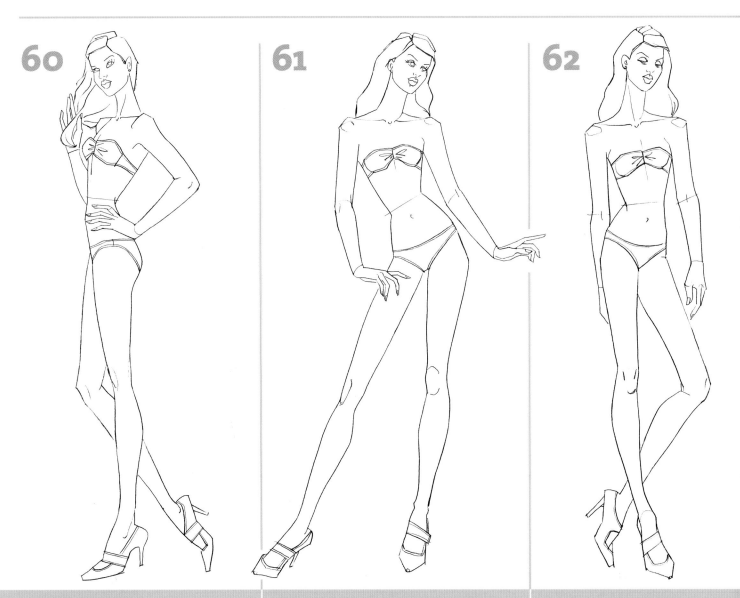

profile view

The arms and hands are elongated to complement the rest of the figure. The play leg is extended behind the model. Note the neck, clavicle, shoulder, elbow, waist, knee, and ankle internal lines, which all define their respective areas. Eliminate all unnecessary lines once your figure is draped, and keep only those that enhance the overall look of your illustration. This pose would be good for a strapless dress fitted through the waist and the hips, flaring toward the knees and worn with a belt.

full front view, dynamic

A classic pose with a slanted hip and tilted head. The model's right leg is the play leg and is drawn longer than the support leg to create balance and a natural posture. Note the three-quarter view of the face with the outline of the cheek visible and part of the model's left eye hidden by the bridge of the nose. This pose would work for an off-the-shoulder dress with waist gathers and horizontal tiers of fabric, or a short dress with a full, flared hem.

full front view

A relaxed pose, with the play leg crossed behind the support leg. The hip and shoulder movements are subtle to allow for the draping of garments without the hindrance of secondary fabric lines and folds. You can see the neck overlap line; be sure to keep this line very light and subtle to keep the neck from looking strained. This pose would be great for a short, empire-waist dress with halter straps and waist gathers or smocking.

The poses in this section could be used with any casual dress. The figures capture a dreamy mood, and have a comfortable and casual stance to complement the style of dresses that will be designed for them. The shoulders are defined and sculpted to enhance strapless dresses and designs with bare shoulders.

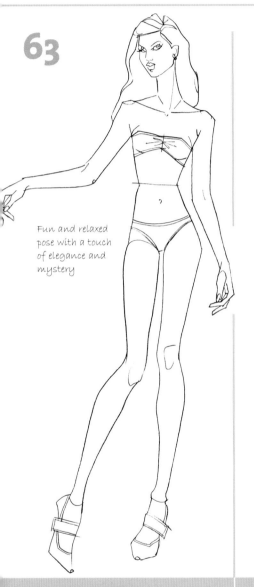

63

Fun and relaxed pose with a touch of elegance and mystery

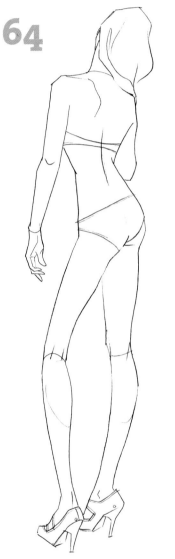

64

full front view, arm extended

The shoulders are slanted in the opposite direction to the hip. The play leg is bent and drawn longer than the support leg. The right hand may be used to hold and lift the edge of the skirt in order to show off its fullness. The model's right leg is rotating inward; note how the knee's overlap line defines the direction of this rotation. This pose would be perfect for a one-shoulder dress with a narrow waist silhouette and flared skirt.

back view

The hips and shoulders are slanted in opposite directions. Most of the model's weight is supported on her right leg. Note how the center back line follows the spine, and the tendon overlap lines behind the knees show the rotation and angles of the legs. When drawing the back of the feet, you can often see a "peek" view of the toes. This pose would be good for a halter dress with straps tied at the back, open-back design, and fitted through the hips.

Zebra-print dress

This figure has been rendered using Adobe Photoshop and watercolor.

The dress is rendered with a woven zebra-print georgette fabric, while the hair and skin are rendered with a mixture of digital and watercolor paints. The dress print covers a large portion of the illustration, providing texture and color variation.

Figure 60 + dress 54

Colors are kept muted and soft; to prevent overcrowding, the ruffles and flounces of the dress are left without color.

Dress:
Day dress

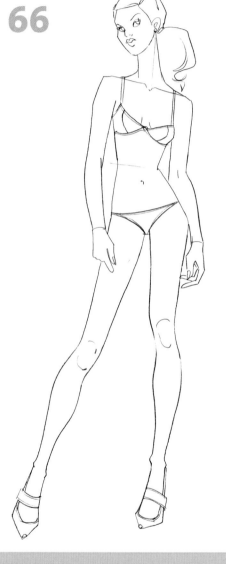

full front view with profile face

A relaxed and elegant stance with subtle hip and shoulder movements. The model's right leg supports most of her weight and the right foot aligns with the balance line. Draw the play leg longer than the support leg to ground the figure on the page. Note the angle of the clavicles, following the slight slant of the shoulders. This would be a good pose for an off-the-shoulder dress with neckline gathers and a trapeze silhouette.

full front view

A classic pose with high hip and low shoulder meeting on the left side of the model. The hands rest comfortably at the sides to complement the casual garments that could be draped on this figure. The model's right hand can be used to hold a purse or pocketbook. This pose would work for a knee-length wrap dress made of light fabric, or a maxidress.

three-quarter view

A comfortable pose with an arm behind the neck. Study the area around the neck and shoulders, keep your overlap lines clean, and be sure each one has a purpose. The face is stretched to the left, giving a three-quarter view. Study the hands and fingers, and note their elongation along with the rest of the body. This would be a great pose for a halter maxidress with skirt gathers and string ties wrapping around an empire waist.

This collection of figures features sexy yet relaxed poses that would complement designs for modern, everyday feminine dresses. Think of the silhouettes that would work with each of the poses: neckline and armhole/sleeve shapes, waist level and fit, hem length and width. Then go in and add design elements such as seams, gathers, and pleats.

Halter maxidress

This figure has been rendered using Adobe Photoshop.

This dress is rendered using large floral eyelet fabric. The garment textile, the skin, and the hair each have their own layer to allow independent manipulation.

 68

69

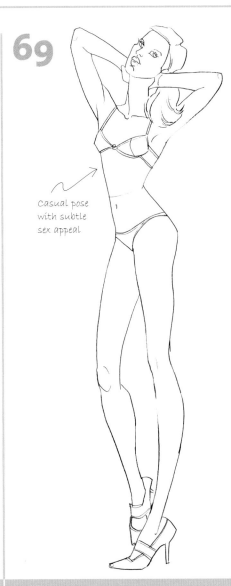

Casual pose with subtle sex appeal

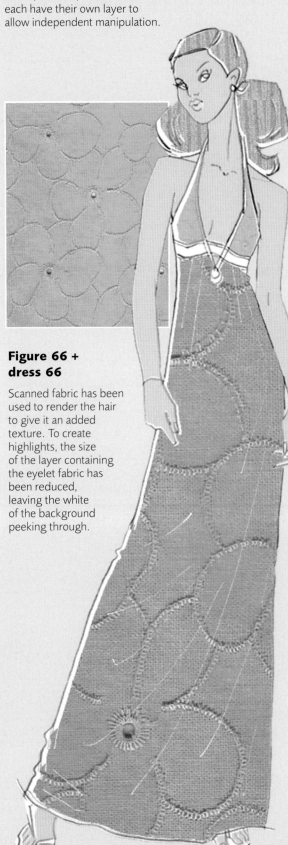

Figure 66 + dress 66

Scanned fabric has been used to render the hair to give it an added texture. To create highlights, the size of the layer containing the eyelet fabric has been reduced, leaving the white of the background peeking through.

full back view

The high hip is connected to the support leg. The play leg extends back and is closer to the viewer, and so drawn longer. The face is only partially visible. The overlap lines play a major role in defining the body; note the jaw, neck, scapula, hip, and knee tendon lines. The back view of the foot is drawn using a circle to depict the heel and a "peek" view of the toes is added. This pose would work for a caped bell-sleeve dress with a dropped back and waist ribbon tie.

three-quarter view, arms behind the neck

Most of the garment details are visible yet the turned pose creates a slimmer silhouette to complement a variety of dress styles. The left leg supports most of the weight and the play leg is bent at the knee. Lightly shade the play leg to indicate depth. This would be a good pose for showing sleeve opening silhouettes, such as batwing armholes or short kimono sleeves. A miniskirt dress with waist smocking and wide armhole openings would be a suitable silhouette.

Dress:
Career dress

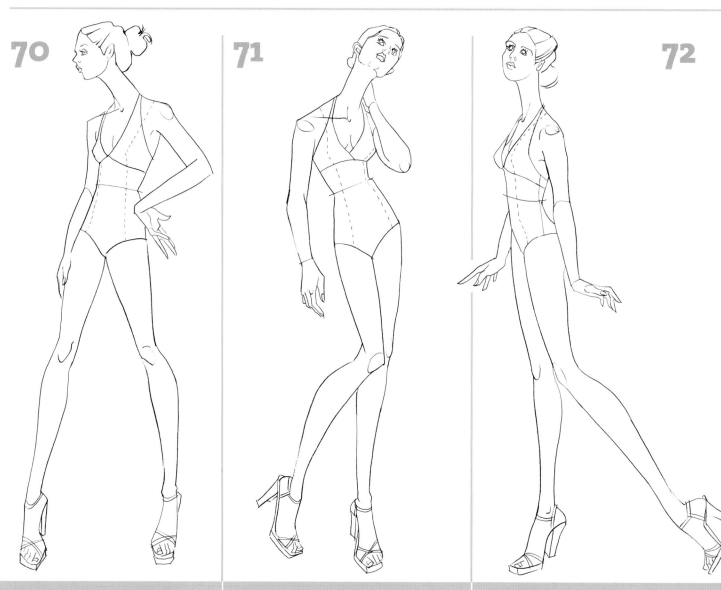

70

71

72

front view, twisted

The weight is equally supported by both legs, giving this figure a robust feel. Study the face profile: draw an imaginary line from the tip of the nose to the chin; note the slope of the line. Extend the chin far away from the neckline for an elegant, feminine look. This would be good for a shirtdress or a deep V-neck A-line dress with bust darts, a wide waist yoke, and flutter sleeves.

front view, dynamic

The hip is shifted to the left and the play leg is bent back on a different plane to the support leg. Note how the overlapping knees create a slim silhouette that opens up toward the feet. The neck, legs, and arms are all elongated to add height and drama. This would be perfect for a 1980s silhouette, such as a two-piece dress with shoulder padding, three-quarter sleeves, deep cowl neck opening, and a fitted skirt worn with a large belt.

profile view

A more feminine stance with neck and play leg elongation. A profile view is excellent for showing silhouettes that are not easily depicted using a front view; use the hands to draw attention to the shape of the garment, such as a dress that fits through the hips and flares at hand level. This would work for a princess-seam dress with puffed sleeves or a shirtdress with bishop sleeves.

These poses express a serious and determined mood while maintaining feminine features and shapes, and can be used for the design of career dresses. Career dresses often have linings and a variety of dart designs to mold the garment around the body. In particular, study dress designs of the 1950s and 1960s, and apply their construction details to your dresses.

Shirtdress

This figure has been draped and rendered using Copic markers on Canson marker paper.

The bold black color of the hair is repeated in the belt and then again in the shoes for unity within the image.

Figure 70 + dress adapted from garments 52 + 85

This is a classic shirtdress with a collar, tailored cuffs, and a buttoned placket, elements that add formality to the look.

73

74

three-quarter view, sitting

The upper torso is straight and the arms are spread apart to show a command of the surroundings. The upper legs are foreshortened because of the seated position. Use this pose to showcase designs that emphasize armhole openings and sleeve designs. It's a great pose for a batwing trapeze dress that narrows at the knee.

three-quarter view

The upper body twists away from the viewer, creating a three-quarter view, while the legs shift to the front-view stance. The movement here is rotational rather than horizontal. Both legs support the weight equally. It would suit a knee-length sheath dress with intersecting bodice darts.

Dress:
Cocktail

The cocktail dress, first named by Christian Dior in the 1940s, refers to a dress worn for semiformal events, ranging from a classy cocktail soirée to a trendy dance club or party. The model's long straight hair, arms stretched above the head, and feet positioned close

75

76

77

three-quarter front view

A dynamic view with the shoulder and hip action lines opposing one another. View the overall figure: draw an imaginary curve from the highest point of the body—the left elbow, connecting to the high hip, down to the knee, and ending beyond the foot. There are several organic curves created by the dynamics of the hips, arms, and legs, which add rhythm and harmony to the pose. Your design and garment silhouette should blend with, and balance, the energetic curves and shapes of the body.

profile view

Most of the model's weight is supported by her right leg, with the support leg closer to the viewer and drawn longer. Study the hand: the upper arm has a relatively simple geometric shape, and the fingers are drawn individually with subtle bends at the knuckles. The neck and arms are elongated to harmonize with the elongated legs.

three-quarter back view

The model is standing relatively straight with both legs supporting her weight. The spine nuance line is visible and follows the center back of the figure. The location of the elbow, hip, and back knee nuance lines help define the angle of view.

to one another all work to create a narrow and slim silhouette, further elongating the body and adding elegance. These figures are suitable for a sophisticated and polished collection of cocktail dresses.

78

79

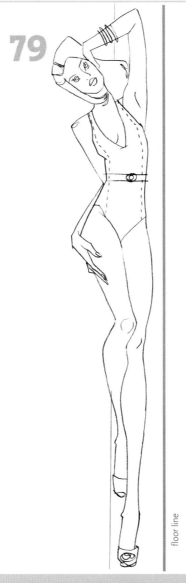

floor line

Long, draping silk charmeuse dress

This figure has been draped and rendered using watercolor on hot press paper.

The skin color is kept light to balance the red dress. Facial features are soft with just enough paint to define them. To render the hair, a mixture of wet brush and dry brush techniques was used. Unless you are making an artistic statement, do not draw dark harsh outlines in the periphery or within the rendered figure.

Figure 78 + dress 64

The sophisticated look of this figure elevates the dress, bringing a level of simple elegance.

front view dynamic figure

The model's right arm is stretched above her head and most of her weight is supported by her left leg. Study the overall dynamics of the figure: draw imaginary curves, starting from the highest part of the figure—the right elbow connecting to the high hip, going through the play knee, and down toward the feet. Note the "S"-shaped curve created by this dynamic. These energetic curves create a more engaging figure.

front view, figure lying with legs overlapping

A less common fashion pose, yet good for depicting a garment's details because the full front view is visible. Study the overall figure: create an imaginary curve by connecting the top of the head to the center of the waist, down to the right foot and beyond. This "C"-shaped organic curve creates a pleasing and natural pose.

Dress:
Clubwear

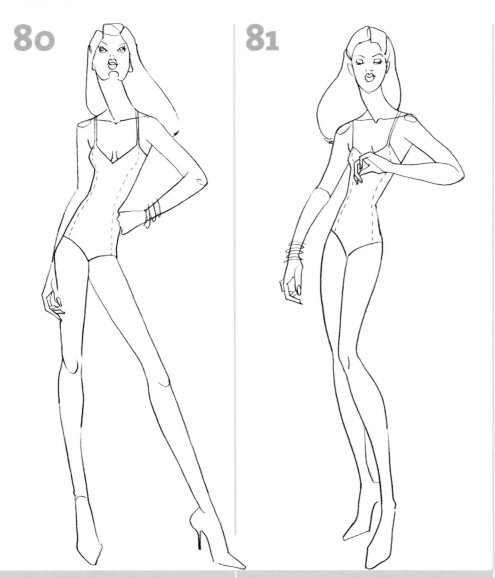

80

81

82

front view, dynamic I

Most of the figure's weight is supported by her right leg. The full front of the design is visible in this pose. It would be perfect for a fitted, bustier minidress with lacing details.

front view, mid-motion

The body is mid-motion, with hip and arm dynamics. Use the lifted arm to display accessories or to divert attention to the waist and hips. This pose would be perfect for a short, fitted, one-shoulder dress with a sheared skirt piece and hem ruffles.

three-quarter front view

The support leg is closer to the viewer and so appears longer. This pose would show off an open-shoulder dress with short batwing sleeves, pleated waistline, and short, A-line skirt piece.

These dynamic figures were developed for modern nightlife dresses. Keep your designs simple—they should be all about silhouette when simple—or layer them with gathers, shears, and pleats for more elaborate creations.

Sequined sheath dress

This figure was rendered using Adobe Photoshop.

This is a modern sheath dress, fabricated with sequins. The model is accessorized with leopard-print gloves and shoes. Highlights are added to the entire outline of the figure to create contrast and brightness.

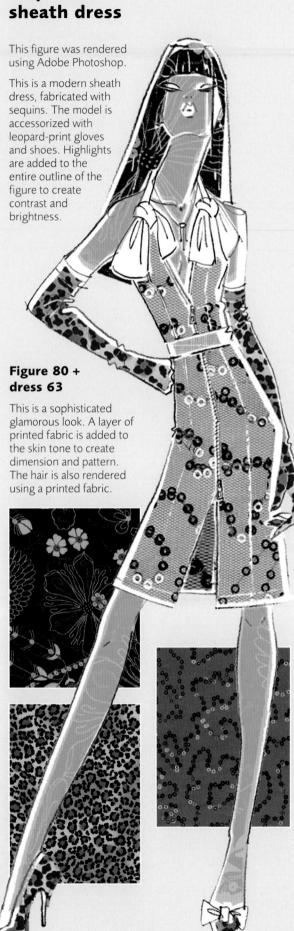

Figure 80 + dress 63

This is a sophisticated glamorous look. A layer of printed fabric is added to the skin tone to create dimension and pattern. The hair is also rendered using a printed fabric.

83

84

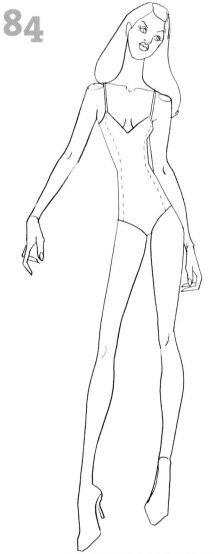

three-quarter front view, bending

This figure has vertical movement, with the upper torso bending toward the ground. Use the animated hands to display accessories, such as bold bracelets, or to open a coin purse—create a story. This pose would be good for a knee-length dress with a plunging cowl neckline.

front view, dynamic II

Most of the figure's weight is supported by her left leg and the play leg extends forward to create a balanced figure. Note the shoulder, hip, knee, and ankle action lines. The shoulder and hip action lines create a dynamic pose while the knee and ankle action lines depict depth. The full front view of the design is visible in this pose. It would work for a boat-neck kimono dress with neckline gathers, fitted at the waist for a trapeze bodice silhouette, flaring toward the hem.

Dress:
Slip dress

85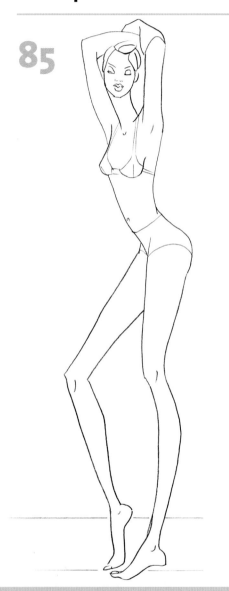

86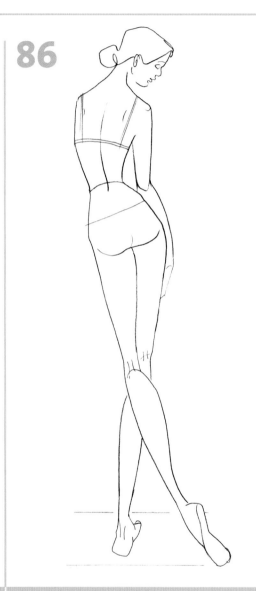

87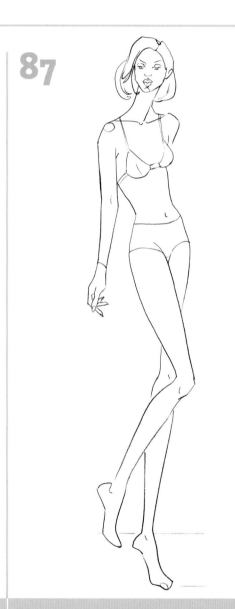

profile view

Both arms resting above the head signals comfort. The model's lower left arm recedes from view and so is foreshortened. The left leg supports most of the body's weight. This would work for a silk halter dress with hem ruffles.

full back view

The hips are tilted to the right and the support leg shifts back toward the balance line at foot level. Note how the internal nuance lines of the scapulae, spine, and posterior knee tendons define the back. Utilize the curvature of the spine and the hips to complement the silhouette of your design. This would be perfect for a draped, long dress with thin straps and back lace detail.

three-quarter front view

A very relaxed pose, with the right foot resting on a platform. It would be good for a boat-neck, kimono-sleeved satin dress with button closure. Use the model's right hand to show off a long, flowing scarf or wrap.

Slip dresses, originally worn under sheer garments, have thin shoulder straps and are bias cut for a soft, relaxed drape. They are casual and comfortable enough to be worn at home for leisure or sleepwear. The focus is on fabric and cut rather than elaborate design elements. These figures have an easy stance with soft body movements.

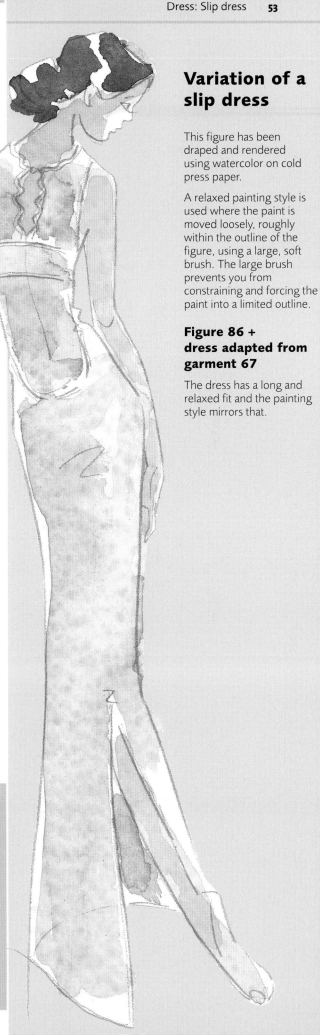

Variation of a slip dress

This figure has been draped and rendered using watercolor on cold press paper.

A relaxed painting style is used where the paint is moved loosely, roughly within the outline of the figure, using a large, soft brush. The large brush prevents you from constraining and forcing the paint into a limited outline.

Figure 86 + dress adapted from garment 67

The dress has a long and relaxed fit and the painting style mirrors that.

88

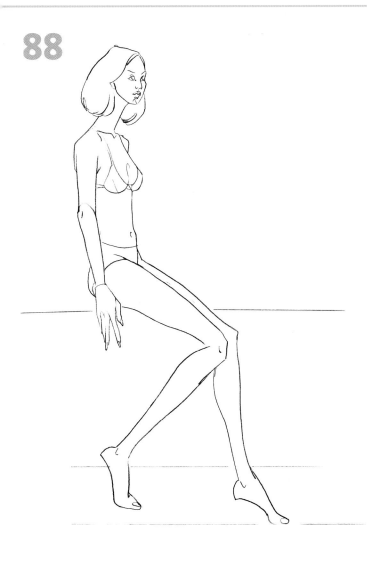

three-quarter view, sitting

A relaxed, contemplative pose, with the hand resting comfortably at the side. Note how the clavicle follows the angle of the shoulder line. This pose would suit a deep, scoop-necked chiffon dress with sheer flutter sleeves and waist gathers.

Outerwear:
Contemporary/junior

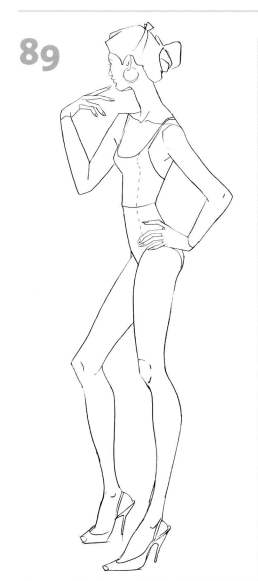

89

90

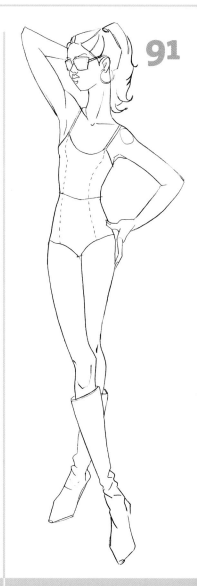

91

profile view

Most of the figure's weight is supported by her left leg, with the play leg bent at the knee. Note how the knee and ankle action lines are slanted to depict that the legs are on different planes. In addition, the model's left foot is drawn slightly larger than her right foot to convey that it's closer to the viewer. Study the contour of the legs: the profile leg is defined around the calf muscles, and is straighter on the side of the tibia. Note how, in a profile view, the neck has a diagonal angle. In this case, it is further elongated to show the face turning away.

front view, dynamic

The shoulder, hip, knee, and ankle action lines have all been exaggerated for compelling effect. Most of the figure's weight is supported on her right leg, and the play leg is drawn much longer to harmonize with the dynamic nature of the pose. Study the arms: the upper arm outline is more defined because of its underlying muscles. The forearm is relatively straighter and narrows toward the wrist. View hands first as "big picture" geometric shapes: the palm and the finger section, then go in and add fingers and details. Use the right hand for accessories, and the left to showcase pocket designs.

front view, dynamic

The shoulder and hip action lines are diagonal, to convey movement. The play leg crosses over the support leg and is closer to the viewer, so it is drawn longer. The knee and ankle action lines are steep, to communicate depth perception. Study the overlap lines of the neck and arm area: they help to define and sculpt the lifted arm.

Outerwear is designed to be worn over other clothing. This is a group of dynamic figures accessorized with earrings, sunglasses, and boots. The poses are suitable for contemporary or junior designs. Use the princess seams on the models as guidelines to accurately place and balance your construction and design elements.

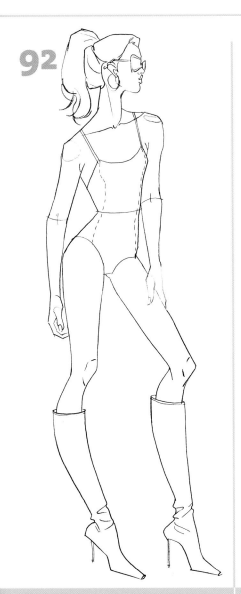

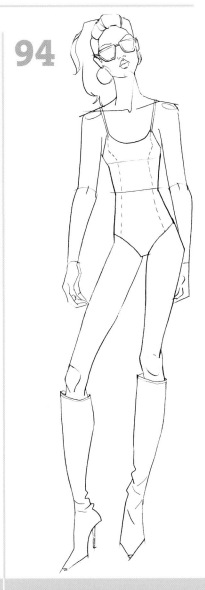

three-quarter front view, dynamic

This figure has rotational movement, with both shoulders turning toward the viewer, while the legs turn away and are visible in profile. The clavicle follows the shoulder action line. Study the arms and the subtle curvature of their outlines. Note how the anterior elbow's overlap lines define the rotation and angle of the arms. Going toward the face and hair, think of hair as shapes rather than individual hair strands.

profile view

Most of the figure's weight is supported by her left leg, and the play leg is closer to the viewer. Study the outline and contour of the chest, hips, and legs in a profile view: the outline curves of one side of the body are distinguishable from the opposite side (contrast the model's linear outline on her right side to that on her left side). Going up toward the neck and face, note the diagonal slant of the neck in profile; this angle creates a natural pose. Study the hand resting on the hips. The fingers are equal in length to the back of the hand. Use the hands to show off pocket designs.

front view, dynamic

The high hip is connected to the support leg, and its corresponding foot aligns with the pit of the neck. The model's play leg is drawn longer to appear closer to the viewer. Going toward the upper torso, the bust volume is depicted by the "break" in the princess seams at the apex level. Study the accessorized face in its front view: the lips are drawn closer to the nose than the chin.

Outerwear:
Designer

95

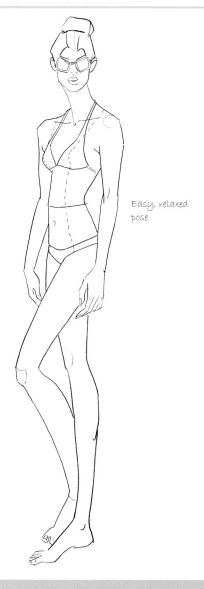

Easy, relaxed pose

96

97

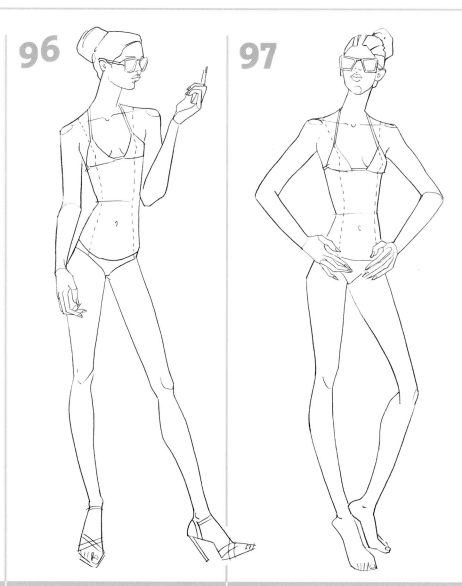

three-quarter front view

A relaxed pose with hands resting at the sides. Most of this figure's weight is supported on her right leg. The knee action line is slanted to convey that the play knee is closer to the viewer. Study the curves and contours of the upper and lower torso: the bust outline becomes visible as the model turns away from view. The location of the belly button can help to define the rotation of the pose; in this case, it is closer to the right side, indicating that the lower torso is turning away from view.

front view, dynamic

Here, the hips and shoulders are slanted, creating diagonal action lines. Most of the body's weight is supported on the right leg. The play leg is drawn longer (note the ankle action line); however, the two legs align at floor level because the play foot is lifted up. The model's left arm may be used to hold a purse, or the hand to hold up a scarf.

front view, shifted left

The hips and shoulders are fairly straight. The left knee is on a lower plane than the right, as it is closer to the viewer. The play leg is bent at the knee; lightly shade the leg's calf (from knee to ankle) to depict this dynamic. Study the shape the arms make. The hands may be placed inside the jacket's pockets to highlight their designs.

These poses are suitable for a designer or formal outerwear collection. Sunglasses may be used to accentuate the tilt and movement of the face. Use the princess seams on the models as guidelines to accurately place and balance your construction and design elements.

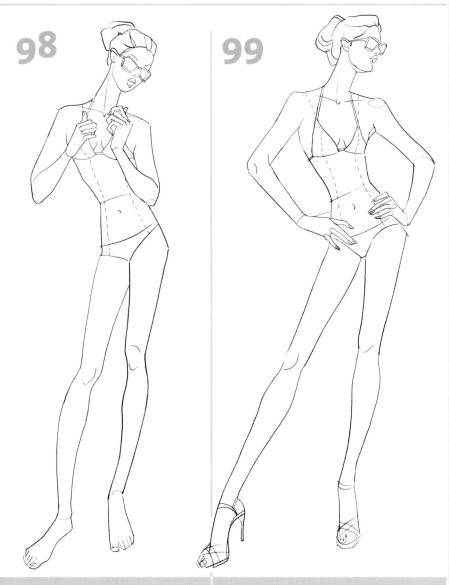

front view, dynamic

Note the exaggerated shoulder and hip movements. The model's support leg is far away from the center front line at the hip level and moves toward it at foot level. The play leg is closer to the viewer and so is drawn longer. Use the hands to hold and display collar designs.

front view, dynamic exaggerated

Draw the shoulder and hip action lines on the figure and note their opposing slopes. Study the arms: the model's right arm and hand are fully visible; her left arm and hand are foreshortened. The right hand is in full view and elongated, with the hand being approximately equal in length to the head.

Denim jacket and tiered skirt

This figure has been draped and rendered using watercolor on cold press paper.

The seams and construction details within the jacket are void of color so that the details are not lost in the rendering. The skirt is made of lightweight cotton and has layers of gathers.

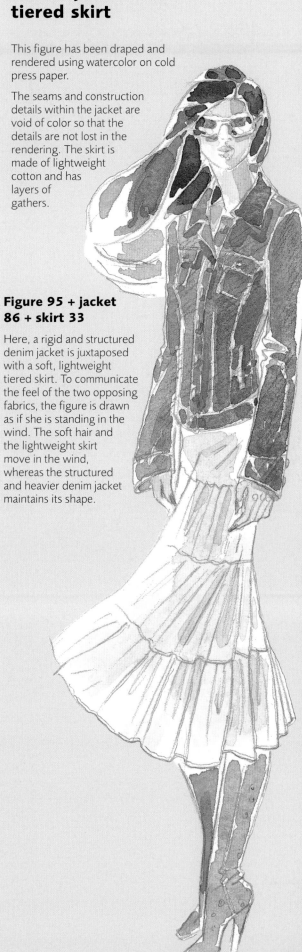

Figure 95 + jacket 86 + skirt 33

Here, a rigid and structured denim jacket is juxtaposed with a soft, lightweight tiered skirt. To communicate the feel of the two opposing fabrics, the figure is drawn as if she is standing in the wind. The soft hair and the lightweight skirt move in the wind, whereas the structured and heavier denim jacket maintains its shape.

Outerwear:
Coats and capes

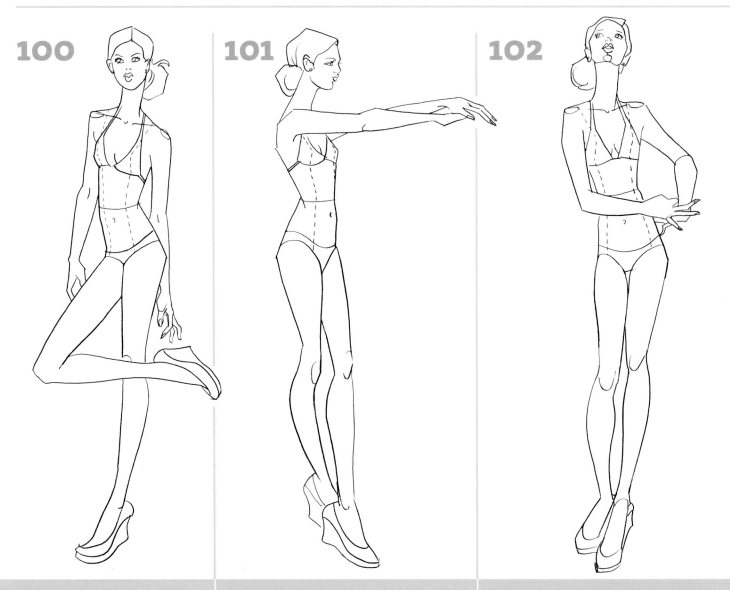

100

101

102

front view, dynamic

The figure's entire weight is supported on her left leg. The hip and shoulder action lines oppose each other to create a bend at the waist. Note that the silhouette is slim on top and widens at the knee; drape your figure to complement this. This pose would suit a belted, princess-seam dressmaker coat with a knee-length pleated peplum and shoulder gathers.

profile view

Most of the figure's weight is supported on her right leg, with the play leg extending beyond the floor line. Study the contour and shape of the profile leg and contrast that to full front legs. Note the diagonal angle of the neck in profile. To create a feminine and elegant pose, pull the neck away from the chin. The arms create a wide silhouette on top and it sharply narrows all the way to the feet. This would be suitable for designs with intricate armhole openings, sleeve and cuff designs, or a knee-length cape with trapeze silhouette, lifted collar, and large patch pockets.

full front view, dynamic

The hip and knee action lines are steep to depict movement and depth perception, respectively. The model's right leg is bent, and her knee is closer to the viewer; lightly shade the calf to show this. Note that the play leg is not always drawn longer; here it recedes from view. The model's left forearm is foreshortened and appears shorter. The face is tilted up and may be depicted by placing facial features on a convex curve, by bringing "up" the lips and nose and drawing them closer to the eyes, and by shortening the forehead. This pose would work for a doubled-breasted trench coat.

Coats and capes are outer garments worn for warmth
and protection. Coats have set-in sleeves and are
longer than hip length. Capes are sleeveless (though
some have slits that act as armholes) and vary in
length. Add elements such as gathers, ruffles, pleats,
and trims for more elaborate and feminine designs.

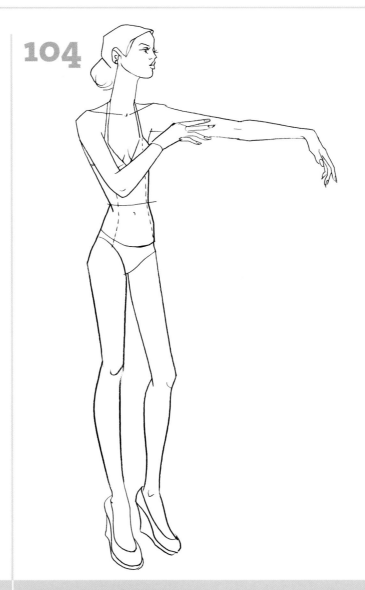

profile view, tilting back

Study the shape and contour of the arms: the back of the
arm is visible and depicted using the elbow overlap line.
The hands merge and the left hand is visible from the
pinkie side. The figure's weight is mostly supported on
her right leg. The play leg is bent and is closer to the
viewer, so it appears longer. Use this profile figure to
show off silhouettes and design elements not otherwise
visible in a front view. It would be perfect for a hooded
poncho or a coat design with interesting cuff detailing.

three-quarter legs

Most of the model's weight is supported on her
right leg, and the play leg is bent at the knee.
Lightly shade the play leg calf to show depth. This
would be good for a long clutch coat open in the
center to partly reveal the legs, draped with a
decorative shawl around the shoulders and arms.

Evening wear:
Prom fantasy

105

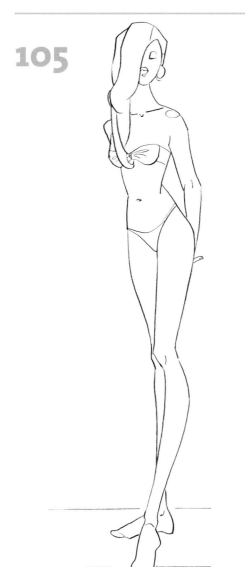

106

107

three-quarter front view

An elegant stance with the hands resting behind the body. The model's legs merge for a slim silhouette. This pose would work for a long, strapless, empire-waist dress with mushroom pleating.

front view

A slim and elegant pose, excellent for showing off a silk-chiffon, one-shoulder dress with shoulder-seam gathers and a wide, gathered waistband.

three-quarter front view

This pose would be great for a typical ball-gown silhouette—a strapless dress with a fitted bodice, full-volume exaggerated skirt, and a large waist bow.

This section covers formal dresses and gowns. The standing poses are simple, with long, loose hair, and are ideal for long, draped dresses. The sitting poses are elegant and sexy, and the leg silhouettes are good for displaying skirts' fullness and embellishments. The closed eyes give the figures an air of fantasy.

Evening dress

This figure was rendered by hand, scanned, and draped and colored using Adobe Photoshop.

The main body of the dress was colored using Photoshop brushes. The color was built up gradually to give a soft flowing appearance to the fabric. Parts of the figure outline were removed to further soften the edges of the dress. The lace was scanned and collaged into the top of the dress; the background of the fabric was removed to leave a transparent ground.

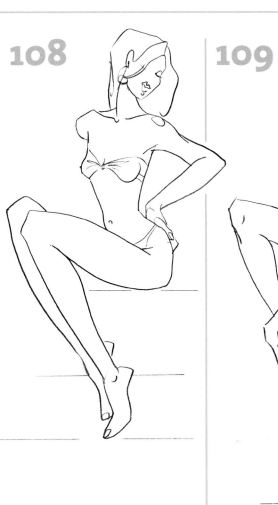

108   109

Figure 106 + dress adapted from garment 67

An elegant evening dress, drawn in a seductive pose, gives a look of sexy glamour.

three-quarter front view, sitting

The shoulders are bent back, creating an upright posture. The arms are stretched back and could be used to show off interesting armholes. The pose would work for a short dress with a boat neck, wide armhole openings, fitted at the waist and flaring toward the hem.

three-quarter front view, reclining

Here, the arms are resting above the head for a refined, sexy design. Use the leg silhouette to show off the fullness of the skirt with tiers of fabric draping the body. This pose would be perfect for a halter dress with a corseted bodice and lace-tiered skirt.

Evening wear:
Bridal dress

110

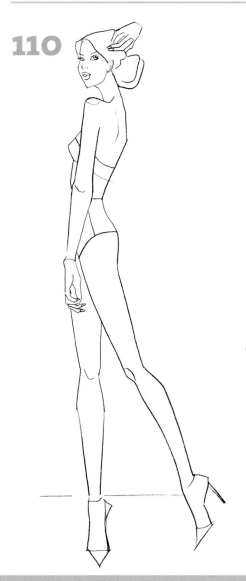

111

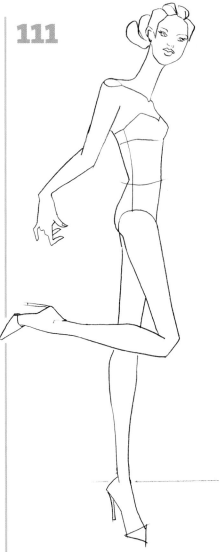

112

profile view

This figure has rotational movement and a playful attitude. The support leg is facing the viewer and the play leg is visible in its profile view. It would be a good pose for a young bride's or bridesmaid's gown, as it shows a partial view of the back upper torso and a train of fabric falling behind the play leg.

profile view, leg lifted

The play leg is lifted up behind the model for an energetic pose. The angle of the clavicle helps to define the tilted shoulder. Use the model's right hand to lift and display skirt designs and fullness. This would be great for a bias-cut, strapless, silk charmeuse dress.

three-quarter front view

Moving up from the hips, the body shifts toward the viewer and turns farther away as it approaches the neck and face. This would suit a short silhouette with a corseted bodice and a pleated or gathered full chiffon skirt.

These poses were created for bridal-related gowns for brides, bridesmaids, and wedding guests. The modern gown silhouette is strapless and long, and with that in mind, these figures have long necklines, alluring shoulders, and elegantly positioned legs to enhance the display of such garments.

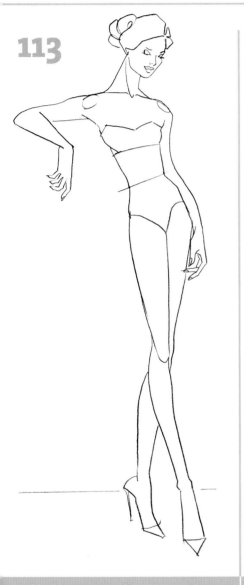

front view

The model's resting elbow creates a wide silhouette at the shoulder line, which narrows as it moves down toward the feet. This pose would work for a long, empire-waist halter dress with accordion pleating and a fairly narrow hem.

three-quarter front view, bending

This figure has vertical dynamics, with the upper torso bending toward the pelvis to expose and emphasize the shoulders and clavicles. It would be great for a full-skirted ball-gown silhouette with a strapless, fitted bodice.

front view, dynamic

Here, the high hip connects to the model's right leg, which supports most of the body's weight. The play leg extends to the left, widening the shape of the pose at foot level, and creating a silhouette that would complement a bridal train draping and falling on the same side. It would be good for a wedding gown with a fitted bodice, loose and soft off-the-shoulder pleated sleeves, and a pleated waistline accentuated by a large ribbon tie flowing on the left side.

Evening wear:
Special occasion

profile views

Profile poses allow you to display garment silhouettes that are not easily depicted in a front view and are more useful here than in any other categories. Use the long and lean upper torso of the profile figures shown here for designs with dropped fitted waistlines, to accentuate this body part and harmonize it with full skirts. To balance the horizontal volume of a ball gown, elongate the legs of your models to add height. Imagine your figures are standing on a platform to display your gowns. Extend the hem beyond the floor level to achieve this vertical extension.

116

117

three-quarter sitting, profile face

The posture is upright and confident. This pose would work for a gown with a corseted bodice and a dropped waistline, and a skirt that flounces and flares, starting at the knees.

profile view

An upright and elegant pose. It would be good for a gown with a low neckline, shoulder and sleeve detailing, dropped waistline, and a full crinoline skirt starting at the hips. Since the feet will be hidden under such gowns, extend the hem lower than the floor level to create a more dramatic silhouette. It's not necessary to change the rest of the proportions.

Evening gowns are all about silhouettes, drape, and fabrics. Drape these figures with gowns of extravagant shapes: think of ball gowns, Victorian bustled gowns, crinoline skirts, and dramatic volumes.

118

Elaborate pose for ball gowns, costumes, historic and cultural gowns

profile view, arms forward

The arms are stretched forward, and the hips are tilted back. This is a stance that would complement an exaggerated Victorian gown silhouette, with most of the garment volume drawn behind the model.

Evening gown with flounce

This figure has been draped and rendered using Adobe Illustrator and Photoshop.

The texture of the gown was rendered using silk brocade and hand-embroidered textiles. The flounce was desaturated to create a mostly grayscale image and to complement the brocade.

Figure 118 + dress 71

The dress has a flounce that adds to the drama of this pose and dress. The flounce was elongated to heighten the drape and silhouette of the gown.

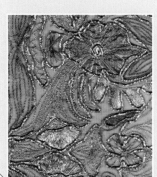

Evening wear:
Formal/semiformal

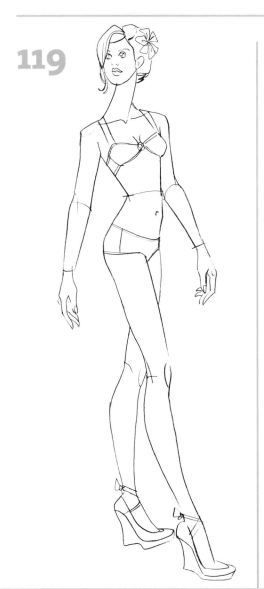

119

120

121

three-quarter view

The upper body twists toward the viewer and legs are seen in profile; the knee overlap lines help to clarify this perspective by being closer to the outline of the knee. This pose would be good for a long georgette dress with off-the-shoulder cape sleeves, fitted and gathered at the waist to create an upside-down triangle silhouette in the upper torso. You can use the leg movement to show slits and openings in the skirt by partly exposing the forward leg. Use the hands to show off clutch purse designs.

front view, crunched

The head is lifted up and the neck elongated to balance the vertical movement of the torso. The model's left leg supports most of her weight, with the play leg bent at the knee and moving forward onto a different plane. In addition to the vertical movement, there is exaggerated side-to-side movement of the hips. Use the dynamic to drape a gown with lots of movement and frills. This pose would be great for an off-the-shoulder gown fitted through the hips and flaring toward the hem.

full front view

The hips are slanted to the left and the corresponding leg supports most of the figure's weight. The play leg is extended beyond the floor line to create balance. If it is drawn shorter than the support leg, your figure will not look grounded and may appear unrealistic, though there are always exceptions to this rule. This pose would work for a halter, empire-waist gown with a skirt overlay opening at center front. Use the arm to lift part of the overlay fabric to display the garment underneath.

These poses would suit a variety of formal events and parties. The figures are sophisticated and sexy, reminiscent of the free-spirited 1970s: think long, flowing kaftans made of satins, chiffons, and georgettes with loose sleeves—kimono- and batwing-style—and long skirts. Render your designs with bold fabric prints and hand embroidery.

122

123

three-quarter back view

The play leg is bent at the knee and is on a different plane than the support leg, creating angled ankle and knee lines. The scapula, elbow, hip, and back knee nuance lines work to define the back area. The center back of the pose naturally follows the spine. The pose would work for a long dress fitted through the hips and flaring toward the hem, with an attached, off-the-shoulder cape overlay.

three-quarter view, sitting

Here, the upper legs are foreshortened. The right hand is resting on a platform and can be used to display sleeve designs. Note the connection and flow between different parts of the figure. The pose would be good for an off-the-shoulder gown with a shirred bodice and long skirt piece, accessorized with a dramatic wrap. Use the crossed legs to display skirt slits, openings, and hem volume, as well as shoe designs.

Swimwear and lingerie:
Casual

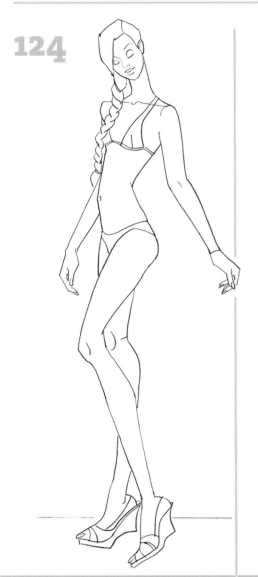

124

125

126

three-quarter front view, turning away

The clavicle defines the angle of the upper torso, and the elbow and knee nuance lines communicate the rotation of the arms and the legs. Use the hands to part skirts or sarongs and display the garment underneath.

three-quarter front view

The twist of the upper body creates a broad shoulder line narrowing toward the waist, exaggerating the shoulder/waist ratio. The model's right arm is foreshortened. The feet are grounded on different planes, with the leg closer to the viewer drawn longer. Study the relationship between different facial features. Draw the lips higher up and closer to the nose. Remember, you are looking up at the model; a common mistake made by beginners is to place the lips too close to the chin.

three-quarter front view, dynamic arms

The movement of the arms here creates a larger silhouette on top, narrowing toward the feet. Your garment's overall silhouette should harmonize with the figure's pose and shape.

These figures have effortless and relaxed poses. The bodies are straight, with light hip and shoulder movements to complement casual designs (contrast these with the figures for "luxury" swimwear on pages 70–71). Here you have maximum skin exposure, and internal nuance lines play an important role in shaping and adding depth to your figures.

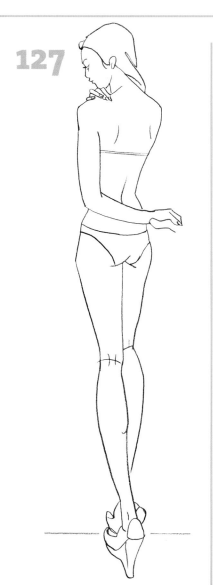

127

128

full back view

One leg is positioned in front of the other, and depth is depicted by the longer left leg as well as the diagonal line of the back knee. The nuance lines of the shoulder, scapula, spine, hip, knee, and ankle define and sculpt the back view.

profile view, arms wrapped

The left leg supports most of the figure's weight and the play leg is closer to the viewer. Overall, a narrow and slim silhouette.

Bikini

This figure has been draped and rendered using watercolor on hot press paper.

To render the skin, a relatively even base color was added to the figure, while leaving small areas of paper untouched to act as highlights. Once the first layer was dried, a very diluted second layer of the original skin color was laid over it. Several bold "color shapes" were added to represent shadows, mainly on the model's left forearm, receding away from view, and the right leg, which is farther away from view.

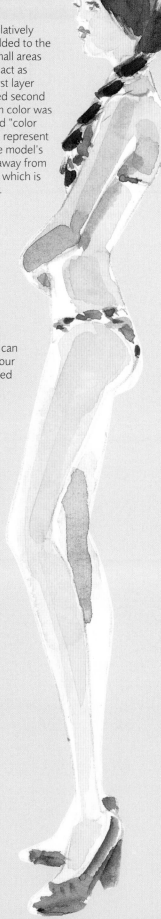

Figure 128 + bikini

A few brush strokes laid down correctly on paper can convey the message of your rendering without the need for cumbersome details.

Swimwear and lingerie:
Luxury

129

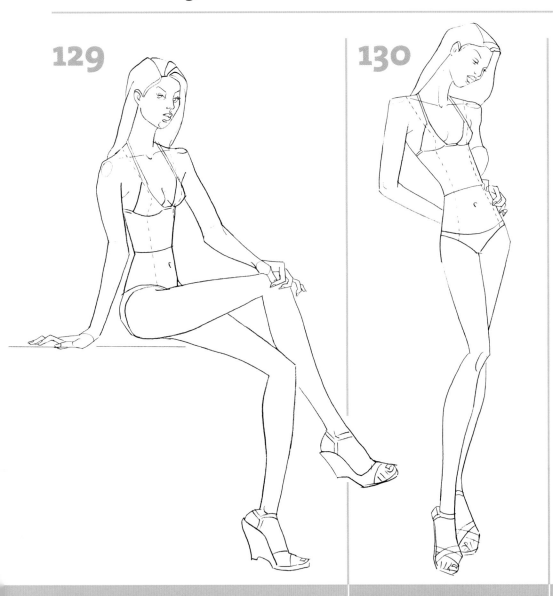

130

131

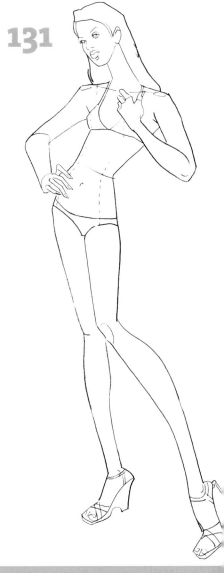

three-quarter front view, sitting

The legs are in motion, mid-crossing. Study the arm and hand resting on the sitting platform and note the "break" that's created at elbow level. The clavicles follow the angle of the shoulder action line. The face is turned for a three-quarter view: the model's left eye is partially hidden by the bridge of the nose. The side of the lip closer to view is fully visible and the other half recedes. This pose would be good for a long robe with butterfly sleevelets draping off the shoulder and a center front opening to display lingerie pieces underneath. Accessorize with large earrings and bracelets.

three-quarter view, dynamic

The hip and shoulder action lines are slanted to depict movement. The left arm is partially hidden behind the model's body and foreshortened. This would work for a trapeze-silhouetted camisole with an empire-waist ribbon tie, worn with low-rise briefs, and accessorized with chains of necklaces.

three-quarter view, dynamic exaggerated

Most of the model's weight is supported on her right leg. The play leg is closer to the viewer and is drawn much longer. In addition, the corresponding foot is drawn larger to emphasize depth. Notice how the angles of the shoulder and hip action lines are exaggerated to create a more dynamic stance. This would be great for a tuxedo-inspired lingerie design accessorized with suspenders.

As a group, these figures have plenty of movement, with twists and turns to make the display of garments more exciting. For a whimsical feel, drape the figures with soft romantic designs in lace and gathered silk chiffons. For a more dramatic collection, clothe them in bold and fancy swimwear and lingerie—pieces with ornate construction, and radiant textiles and embellishments.

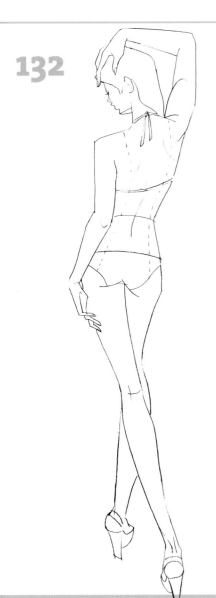

132

133

full back view

The hips are slanted to the left and the right arm is lifted to balance the stance. Note the use of overlap lines in the shoulder area and scapula to add dimension and define the lifted arm. Other nuance lines are the elbow, hip, back of the knee, and Achilles tendons. The center back of the body naturally follows the curve of the spine. The ankle action line is highly slanted to communicate that the model's left leg is closer to the viewer. Study the feet: in the back view, you can see the ball of the feet with a "peek" view of the toes. Use this pose for a racer-back bra and hip-huggers with center-back gathers.

three-quarter front view, arms lifted

The silhouette is broad on top where the arms rest on the head, and narrows toward the feet. Most of the model's weight is supported on her left leg and the right leg is slightly bent at the knee (note the knee action line). Lightly shade the calf to depict this bend. This pose would work for a long, sheer, chiffon, empire-waist robe worn over undergarments. Accessorize with bold earrings and necklaces.

Active sportswear:
Fitness

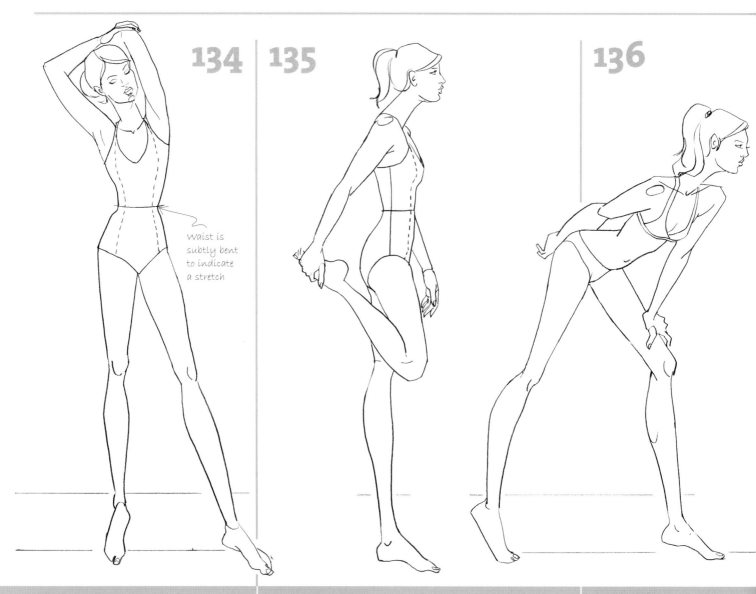

134 | 135 | 136

Waist is subtly bent to indicate a stretch

full front view

Most of the figure's weight is supported on her right leg, with the play leg extending beyond floor level. The arms and upper torso are stretched, creating a bend at the waist on the opposite side.

profile view

Here, side seams of garments will be fully visible, along with the right princess seam. All of the body's weight is supported on the left leg. The play leg is lifted up by the arm. Only half of each feature is visible: half of one eye, shaped like a horizontal "V," the bridge of the nose, and half of the lip, shaped like a horizontal heart. Place the eyes near the groove where the forehead and nasal bridge meet. Draw an imaginary line from the tip of the nose to the bottom of the chin and note its slant. Also note the diagonal angle of the neck in profile; the neck should not stand upright in a profile view or your figure will appear strained and unnatural.

profile, bent pose

This figure has vertical (up and down) movement. The model's left arm resting on the leg supports the weight of the upper torso. The right arm is foreshortened.

This category can include garments for broad activities from swimming and tennis, to dance. The clothing is as varied as the activities. The common thread is functionality and practicality. These figures have movement and body stretch to reflect the dynamic nature of the garments.

137

138

front view, dynamic

The shoulder action line has a steep slope created by the stretching action of the arm. By exaggerating the slope of your action lines, you can create highly dynamic poses.

three-quarter front view

This sporty figure is standing with both legs supporting her weight. The face is turned away, while the upper torso twists toward the viewer. The figure is stretching a bit and has a strong energetic vibe.

Menswear:
Classic

139

140

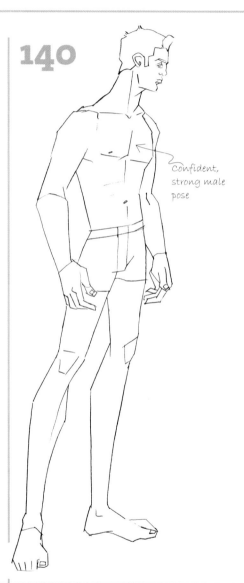

*Confident,
strong male
pose*

141

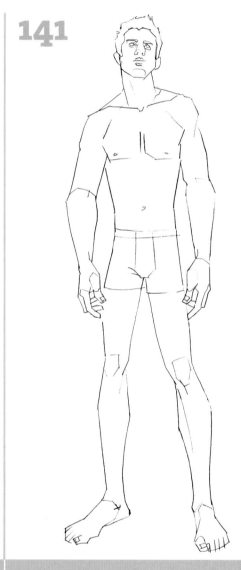

profile view

The shoulders and upper torso are shifted back and the face is turned up, signaling confidence and strength. The hand on the waist may remain there or be placed inside the garment's pockets.

three-quarter
front view

Both legs support the weight of the figure. Angular lines and larger hands add to the masculine feel. If you find your male faces look feminine, a simple trick is to eliminate the upper lip altogether.

full front view

This male figure, with hands away from the body, is ideal for showing clothing without any hindrances. Both legs support the weight of the body.

These are idealized male figures. Men's figures are 9–10 heads long, similar to women's figures; however, because of the broader shoulders and overall width of the male body, they do not appear to be as long. Do not exaggerate the length of male legs, otherwise they appear too feminine. Male figures frequently support their weight on both legs, so there is less movement in the hips.

142

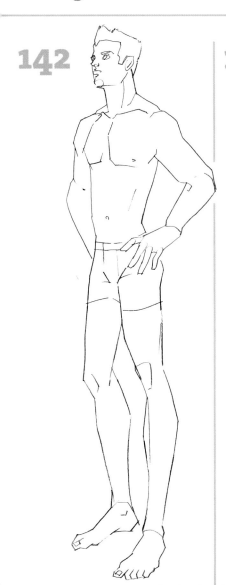

143

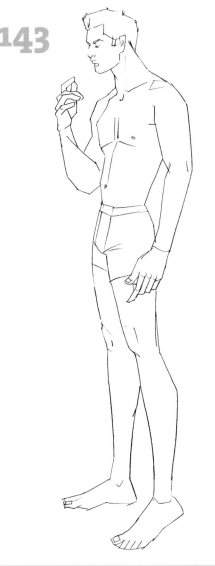

144

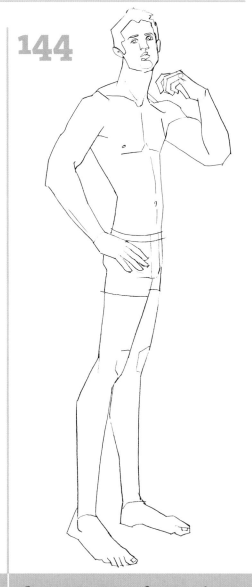

three-quarter front view, head up

This figure's head is tilted up to communicate confidence, yet the pose is relaxed and approachable. The hands may remain on the hip or be placed inside a jacket or pants pocket.

three-quarter front view, relaxed

Note the weight of the body being supported equally on both legs. The lifted hand may be used to draw attention to specific garment parts, such as a necktie or scarf.

three-quarter front view, lifted arm

In general, the hands are less conspicuous in men's poses, unless they serve a purpose. For example, in this case, they could be used to hold a jacket or suit over the shoulder. The right hand can be placed inside the pocket for a sophisticated look.

Menswear:
Casual/sportswear

145

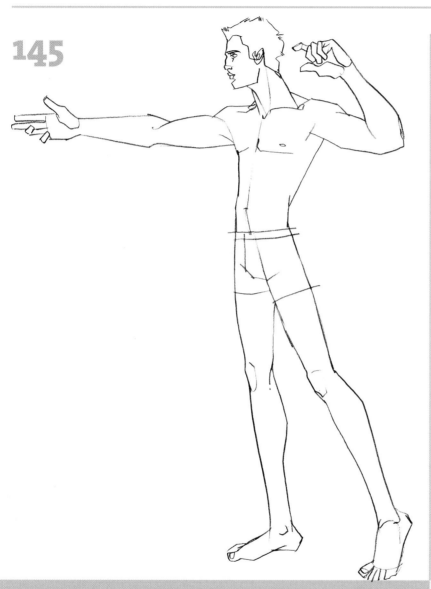

146

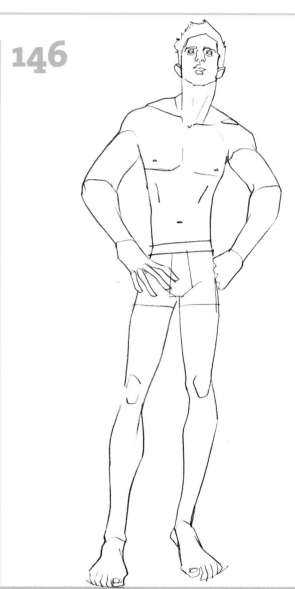

three-quarter front dynamic figure with a profile view of the face

Most of the weight of the pose is supported by the right leg. Study the neck and shoulder area: the overlap lines in this region add depth and dimension to the figure. Study the overall silhouette of the figure: the shoulders are broad and the stretched arm exaggerates this width, the waist and hips are narrow and straight, with the play leg stretched behind the body. Follow the "C"-shaped curve that's created, starting at the pit of the neck, passing through the belly button, all the way down to the extended left foot (play leg). This organic curve creates a balanced and harmonious stance. Study the profile face: note the pronounced nasal bridge and the structured and angular chin, and the hairline, creating a masculine figure.

full front view

A casual and confident pose. The shoulder has a dynamic action line opposing the subtle hip tilt. The model's play leg extends forward and is closer to the viewer. To show this depth perception, the play leg is drawn longer than the support leg (left leg). Note the clavicle, shoulder, and elbow overlap lines, adding depth and dimension to the figure.

To make your figures masculine, play with line quality and angles. By making the contour of the face and body more angular, increasing the size of the hands and feet, and by widening the neck, the figures will take on a stronger, more masculine shape. Adding a few concise overlap lines helps to define and sculpt the body and adds depth to the figure. Men have thicker, lower-set eyebrows, a more pronounced nasal bridge, and angular jaw lines.

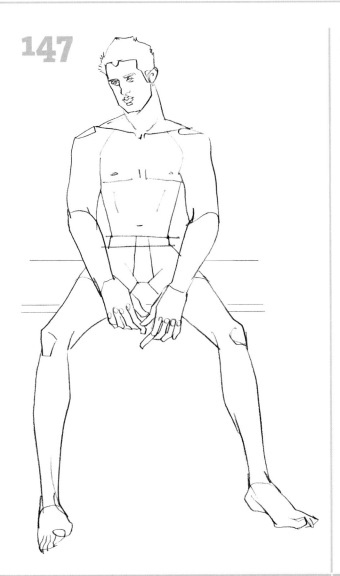

147

148

front view sitting pose

A casual and pensive pose. Study the overall figure: the neck is wide, the shoulders broad, and the hands enlarged for a masculine feel.

profile figure with the upper body twisting toward the viewer

Study the face: note the eyebrows are thicker and closer to the eyes, the lips thinner in comparison to the female, and the jaw line structured and angular.

2

Basic garment blocks

For the most part, the garments in this section show accurate and detailed designs. Various design elements, as well as fabric folds and drape lines, have all been accurately depicted. They were drawn to clearly communicate the design, fit, and drape to those in the fashion industry. They are basic, everyday garments, from which you can develop more elaborate designs.

The garment can first be viewed in its overall silhouette or shape. For instance, compare the shape of a pencil skirt versus a trumpet skirt. Within the silhouette, many details are added that are both functional and aesthetic. These details are the design elements of clothes.

Design elements can be organized into three broad categories:

1 Construction design elements, including: seams and stitching to hold fabric pieces together; folds in fabric to mold it to the body and to create design variety, for example, darts, tucks, pleats, gathers, ruffles, cascades; and finally, garment pieces such as collars, cuffs, pockets, and plackets.

2 Trims and accessories, which includes closures and fasteners, such as buttons and zippers, any trimmings and lacings, ribbons, and pieces that are added to the garment.

3 And finally, the garment's textile inherently creates design variation. Different prints, such as stripes or animal prints, and textures, such as velvet or satin, add dimension to the garment and provide functional and aesthetic diversity.

Clockwise from the top left:
Collection by Sylvia Kwan;
figure by Nanae Takata; figure
by the author; figure by
Tracy Turnbull.

Tops:
Fitted tops

1

Side seam

Drape folds

2

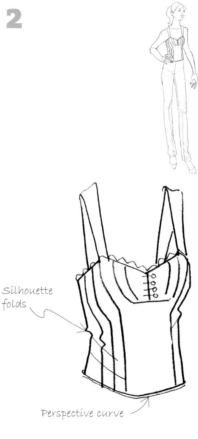

Silhouette folds

Perspective curve

3

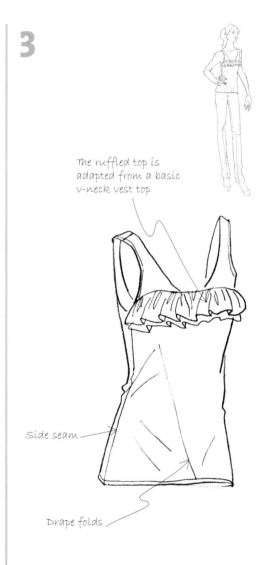

The ruffled top is adapted from a basic v-neck vest top

Side seam

Drape folds

basic top

A simple sleeveless vest top forms the basic block for a range of other tops. Use knit fabric for a figure-hugging wardrobe essential.

bustier

In woven fabric, with seaming to give a tight fit and structure, this bustier top features a front buttoned yoke detail and scalloped edging. Here, it is shown with wide straps; you could use spaghetti straps or make it strapless.

ruffled top

The basic vest top is here given a double ruffle detail above the bust. You could make the ruffles in the same fabric as the top, or use a contrast knit or woven fabric.

A basic vest top is the starting point for a variety of short- and long-sleeved tops in a range of knit and woven fabrics, with a variety of embellishments from ruffles and butterfly sleeves to capes.

4

5

Gathers

Drape folds

pintucks and butterfly sleeves

This high-necked top would work in a light woven fabric. It has a pintuck detail at the front, princess seams, and pretty butterfly sleeves.

cape-collar top

This variation on the basic top has a built-in mini "cape," which gives the effect of sleeves. The cape is finished at the front with a bow-tie neckline. Try woven or knit fabric, depending on the effect you would like to achieve—stiff and formal, or softer and more relaxed.

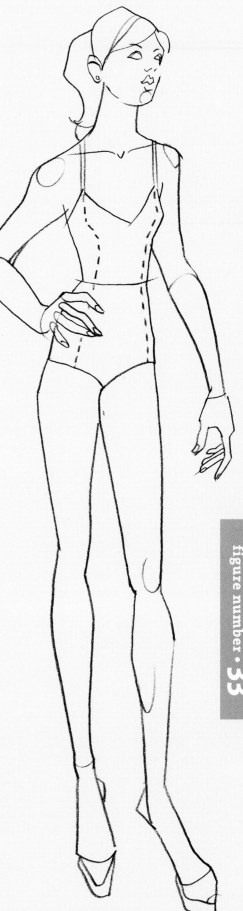

figure number • **33**

Tops:
Knits and woven

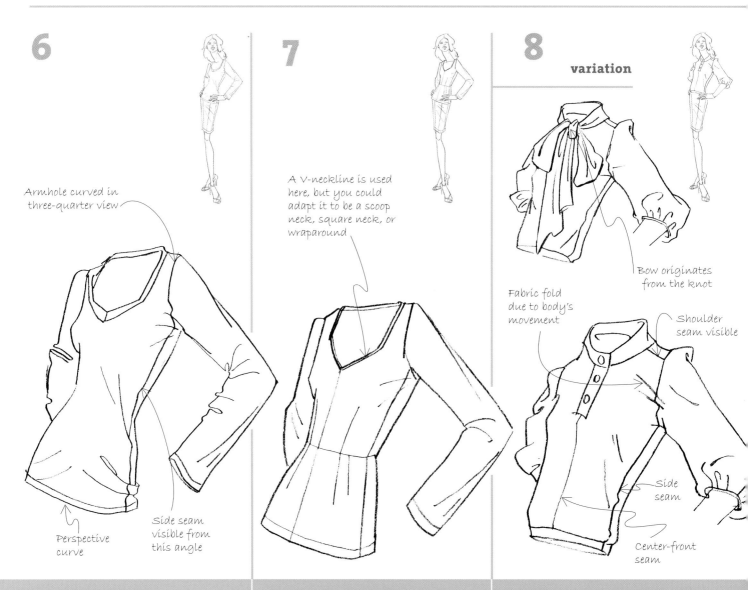

6

Armhole curved in
three-quarter view

Perspective
curve

Side seam
visible from
this angle

7

A V-neckline is used
here, but you could
adapt it to be a scoop
neck, square neck, or
wraparound

8

variation

Bow originates
from the knot

Fabric fold
due to body's
movement

Shoulder
seam visible

Side
seam

Center-front
seam

knit fitted top
This design hugs the body, courtesy of
the slinky knit fabric and careful cut. The
soft fabric folds and molds itself to the body
as it bends. It is the basic block for a range
of adaptations.

woven fitted top
The same design but in a rigid, woven fabric
requires darts to mold the fabric to the
body's contours. Seaming adds structure
and visual interest. The neckline or sleeve
shape could be varied.

banded-collar blouse
This more formal blouse features a banded
collar and buttoned placket fastening, with
center-front seam. Cropped bishop sleeves
make a strong statement and accentuate the
lower arms.

These tops show how a basic shape can be adapted through the use of carefully chosen detailing and fabric types. A basic, close-fitting knit or woven top can evolve into more elaborate formal or casual styles as desired.

9

Looped strap

Side seam

Perspective curve

10

Fabric folds created by gathers

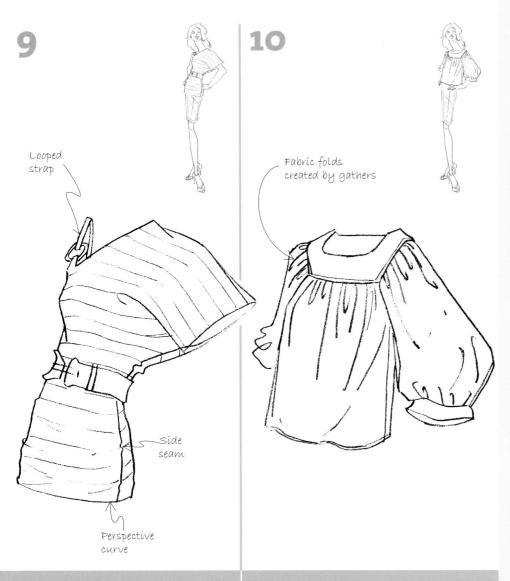

unishoulder tunic

This asymmetrical garment is supported on the right side by a looped strap and has a single kimono-style sleeve. The horizontal stripes contour the body and act as an additional design element.

peasant top

A woven or knit peasant top may be casual or formal, depending on the choice of fabric. The body of the top is gathered at the shoulder and neck yoke, and into banded cuffs on the sleeves, creating a pretty, feminine silhouette.

Tops:
Using gathers

11

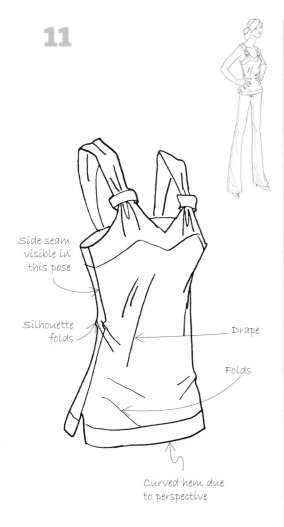

Side seam visible in this pose

Silhouette folds

Drape

Folds

Curved hem due to perspective

12

Smocking

Side seam visible

Perspective curve of hem

13

variation

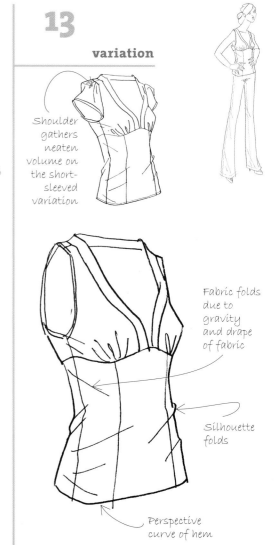

Shoulder gathers neaten volume on the short-sleeved variation

Fabric folds due to gravity and drape of fabric

Silhouette folds

Perspective curve of hem

basic top with strap gathers

This very simple top is enlivened by the strap detail, with gathers at the front, just above the bust. The fabric drapes from the bust to small side slits at the hem. This design would work in woven or knit fabric.

smocked top

This variation on the basic top features a broad band of smocking at the waist. Smocking is the term used to describe the three parallel rows of gathers. This would work with woven or knit fabric.

fitted bodice with bust gathers

This fitted style would suit a lightweight, woven fabric. Bust gathers are drawn into the tight, princess-seamed bodice. Two versions are shown here—one sleeveless and the other with short sleeves and shoulder gathers to neaten the volume.

Gathers are used to create volume, ruffles, shirring, and smocking. Depending on where you place gathers, you can achieve a range of exciting effects, as this selection of tops demonstrates.

14

variation

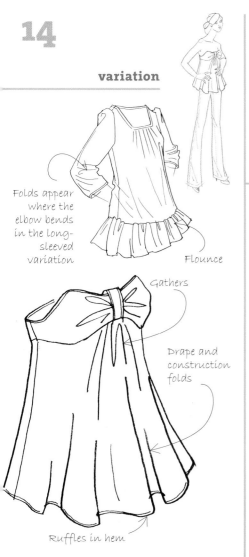

Folds appear where the elbow bends in the long-sleeved variation

Flounce

Gathers

Drape and construction folds

Ruffles in hem

15

variation

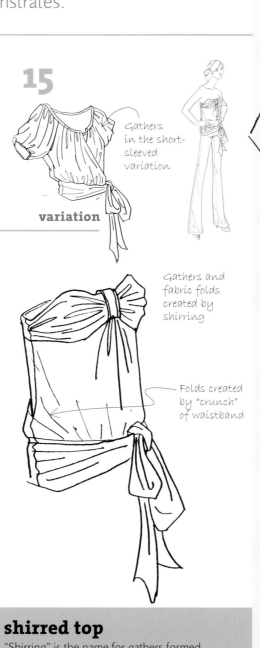

Gathers in the short-sleeved variation

Gathers and fabric folds created by shirring

Folds created by "crunch" of waistband

strapless ruffled top

Gathers around the bust of this strapless top add definition; below the bust, the top flares out to a ruffled hemline. A long-sleeved variation is also shown here, with a square neckline and a deep flounce at the hem. You could work this design in woven or knit fabric, depending on the effect you want to achieve.

shirred top

"Shirring" is the name for gathers formed on two parallel seams; here, the shirring is over the bust on the strapless version, and at the asymmetric waist tie, which is finished by a large bow. The short-sleeved, shirred top has gathers at the neckline, sleeve hems, and waist.

figure number · 31

Sleeves:
Short

16

variation

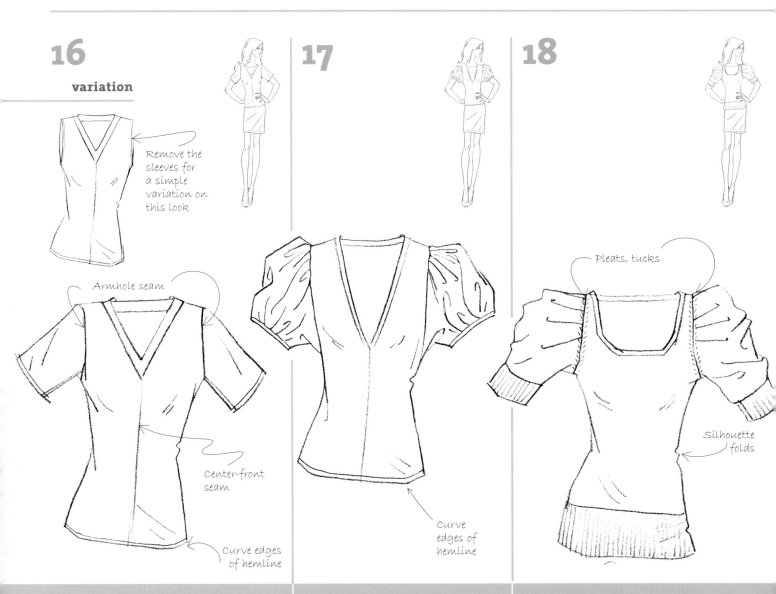

Remove the sleeves for a simple variation on this look

Armhole seam

Center-front seam

Curve edges of hemline

17

Curve edges of hemline

18

Pleats, tucks

Silhouette folds

short, fitted sleeves

A fitted, knit T-shirt with simple, set-in sleeves and a center-front seam; different necklines can be added to create a variety of designs. This block is a versatile basic that may be adapted to suit casual or formal occasions.

puff sleeves

A more elaborate variation on the basic knit T-shirt theme; this top features shoulder and armhole gathers, extending the fabric above shoulder level for a sumptuous, dramatic effect. Keep the neckline simple to avoid detracting from the sleeve detail.

pleated sleeves with rib knitting

A pretty, feminine treatment for a simple knit top. Generous pleats at the armhole seam form voluminous sleeve tops, tapering neatly into a rib cuff just above the elbow.

A basic, short-sleeved top can be adapted almost endlessly—from the classic fitted T-shirt, suited to almost any occasion, to more structured, dressy garments with sculptural sleeve details in a range of woven and knit fabrics.

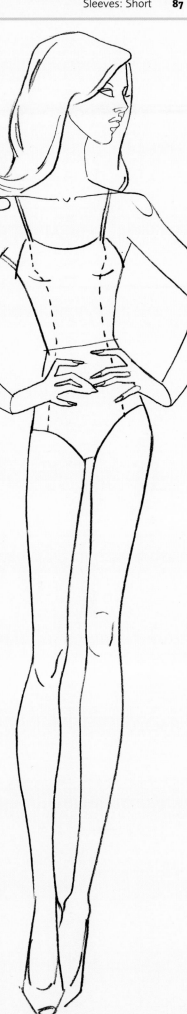

19

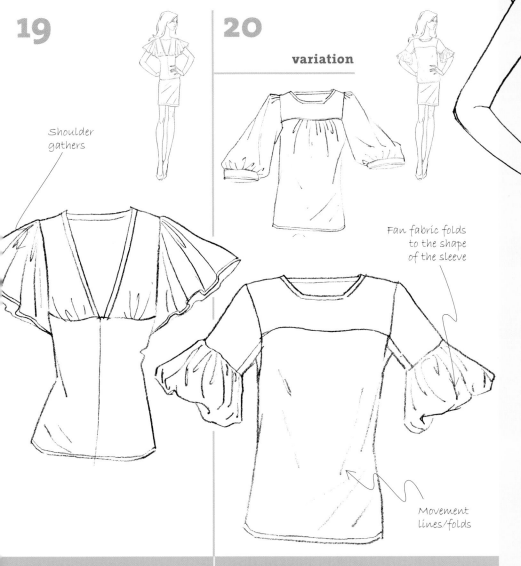

Shoulder gathers

20

variation

Fan fabric folds to the shape of the sleeve

Movement lines/folds

circle sleeves with gathers

This elegant top features gathers at the shoulders and bust, allowing it to drape beautifully around the body. The floaty sleeves form a profusion of ruffles created by both the gathers and the circular cut of the fabric.

bubble sleeves

This more structured, directional top employs a number of features. The sleeves end in a round "bubble" hem, with gathers to create plenty of volume. The body of the garment falls from an armhole yoke above bust level and drapes around the body. A variation with gathers below the yoke and full, puffed sleeves with shoulder gathers is also shown here.

Sleeves:
All-in-one

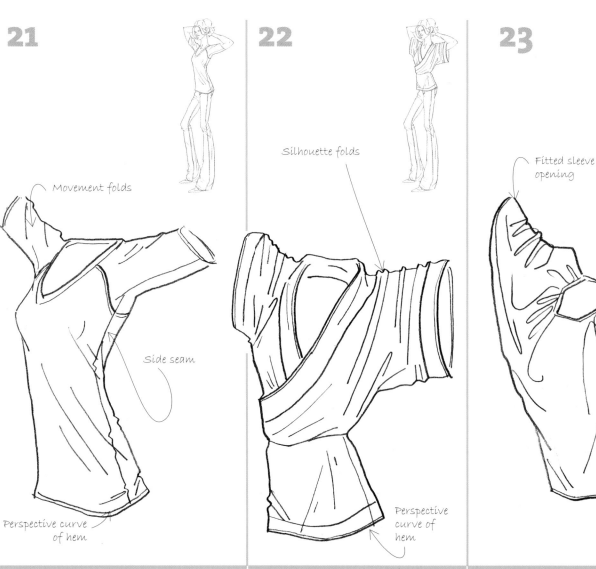

21

Movement folds

Side seam

Perspective curve
of hem

22

Silhouette folds

Perspective
curve of
hem

23

Fitted sleeve
opening

Loose here

raglan sleeves

The raglan sleeve armhole connects to the neck opening (as opposed to a set-in sleeve, where the armhole is positioned away from the neck opening). You could use knit or woven fabric for this type of sleeve.

kimono sleeves

This top may be made in woven or knit fabric, and features deep kimono sleeves with loose armholes and large sleeve openings. Kimono sleeves are an example of all-in-one sleeves, where the sleeve and bodice are cut in one piece and there is no armhole seam.

batwing dolman sleeves

This top may also be woven or knit, and again has all-in-one sleeves, where the sleeve and bodice are cut in one piece and there is no armhole seam. The armhole is wide and the sleeve narrows toward the wrist. It also has neck gathers, and the sleeves are tight at the cuffs, creating an entirely different silhouette.

The tops shown in this set are all designs with sleeves that incorporate the bodice. Here, tops are shown, but you could also apply these sleeve designs to dresses.

24

25

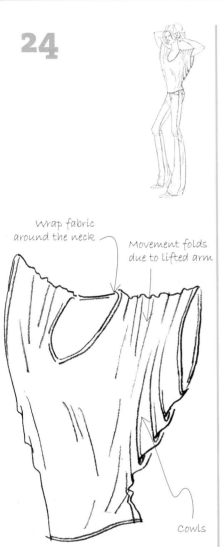

Wrap fabric around the neck

Movement folds due to lifted arm

Cowls

Perspective curve

cowl sleeves

This top, again with all-in-one sleeves, makes use of a cowl construction to cause the fabric to drape beautifully. Experiment with woven or knit fabrics for different effects.

cape sleeves

Another variation on the all-in-one sleeve, this top gives the effect of a cape when seen in silhouette. The sleeves and the bodice are cut together.

figure number · **14**

Skirts:
Fitted and A-line

26

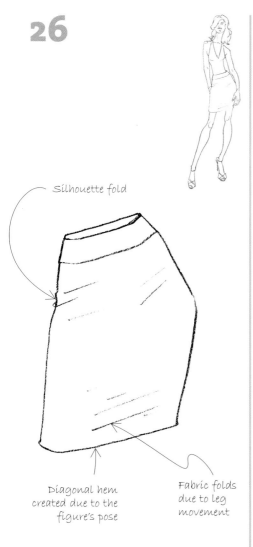

Silhouette fold

Diagonal hem created due to the figure's pose

Fabric folds due to leg movement

27

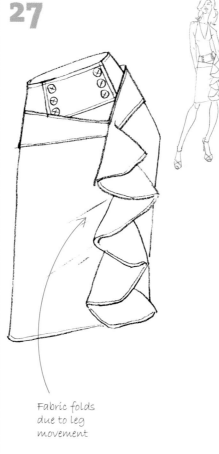

Fabric folds due to leg movement

28

Gravity lines

Center front

basic fitted skirt

This deceptively simple skirt is cut close to the body. The perfection of the cut is paramount, and the choice of fabric—which may be knit or woven—is critical to the effect of the finished garment.

cascaded pencil skirt

Here, a basic woven pencil skirt is enlivened through a cascade detail at the front, which adds movement and direction. The buttons on the right are functional, while the ones on the left are decorative and are placed to balance the design.

basic A-line skirt

A classic woven A-line skirt is tapered into the flat waistband with a few neat darts. The extra fabric in the skirt creates more movement than the straight version and drapes pleasingly around the legs.

Fitted skirts—a timeless and flattering fashion staple—lend themselves to many variations, with volume and drama being added in the form of pleats, godets, and cascades. Even a simple A-line cut makes an otherwise straightforward and serious skirt more flirty and fun.

29

Uneven line to show skirt opens here

Lines due to gravity's pull on the fabric

30

variation

Pleated flounce

Fabric folds due to the tension created by the leg movement

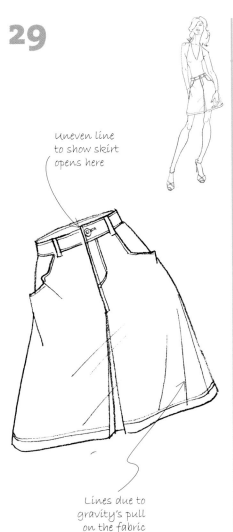

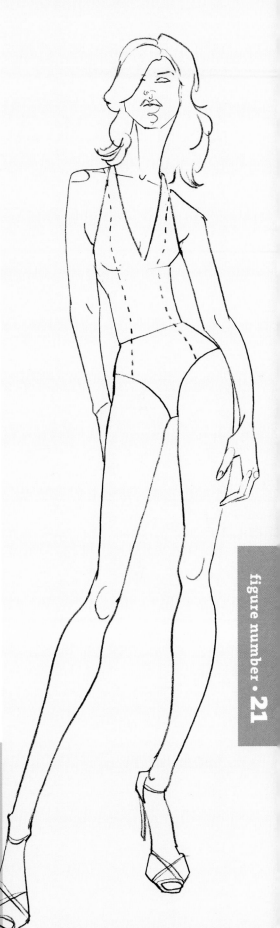

denim A-line skirt

A basic A-line skirt is worked in denim and given jeans styling: zippered and buttoned fly, reinforcing, double topstitching in a contrast color, and continental pockets. This particular design also features an inverted pleat.

godet skirt

This skirt is fitted to the knee and flared below. Panels mold the skirt around the body, and godets between the panels add volume, for an almost "fishtail" effect. This type of design works in woven or knit fabrics, for a more structured or a softer effect, respectively.

Skirts:
Longer and ruffled

31

Silhouette folds

Fabric lines due to body's movement

32

Lines due to movement and drape of fabric

33

Tier seams

fitted skirt

A simple, fitted skirt in a woven fabric requires long darts to mold it to the body at the deep waistband. The movement of the legs creates the effect of a diagonal hemline, though it is in fact cut straight.

wrap skirt

This wrap skirt is finished with a soft, wrapped waistband and a cascading ribbon tie. The skirt has an asymmetric opening, allowing for freer movement of the legs, despite the skirt's long, slim silhouette.

tiered skirt

This skirt creates a dramatic, full silhouette, falling in three gathered tiers to the floor. The covered drawstring waistband is finished with a simple tie. Vary the number and width of the tiers and the length of the skirt for a range of possible moods.

Skirts lend themselves to all kinds of creative expression in terms of shaping. A simple, fitted skirt acts as a basic block for wrap, tiered, or ruffled and layered variations. Try luxury fabrics for instant evening glamour. Play with different lengths, too, from maxi to mini.

34

Create uneven side seams to show layers

Gathers

35

Gathers

Ruffled hem

figure number • **33**

lightweight layered skirt

Choose fabrics such as tulle or georgette for this fabulous, playful design. Myriad ruffles are created by the gathered layers of fabric. The overall effect is irregular and undefined, with striking volume. Knit fabrics would work, too, for a more relaxed effect.

medium-weight layered skirt

A more substantial woven fabric is used here to create a structural, "stacked" effect. This skirt design stands away from the body and would need to be balanced by a fitted top.

Pants:
Front view

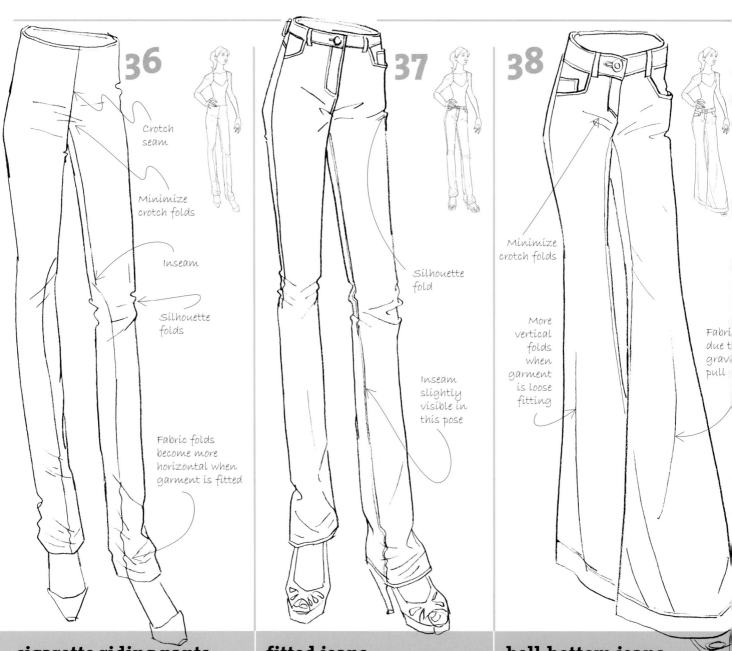

36

Crotch seam

Minimize crotch folds

Inseam

Silhouette folds

Fabric folds become more horizontal when garment is fitted

37

Silhouette fold

Inseam slightly visible in this pose

38

Minimize crotch folds

More vertical folds when garment is loose fitting

Fabri due t grav pull

cigarette riding pants
These long, slim pants feature a twist on a classic shape, courtesy of the curved "riding"-style seams at the lower leg. Choose woven or knit fabric, depending on your desired effect—fitted and sculptural or super figure-hugging.

fitted jeans
These basic jeans feature classic western styling: continental pockets, zipper stitch lines, and a small "coin" pocket. Notice how the belt loops are placed equidistant from the center-front. This style would suit a woven fabric, but it doesn't have to be denim—use your imagination!

bell-bottom jeans
These jeans look like the basic model at the top with their pockets and stitching details, but are cut for maximum drama as they approach the hemline. Wide flares of heavy woven fabric retain their shape and volume, and end in a rounded hem, creating a distinctly retro silhouette.

The basic pants silhouette is open to a range of interpretations. Start long and lean, then play with proportions—from fitted jeans, to bell bottoms, to extravagant harems. The fabric choice is all-important here, determining the drape and fit—where the pants cling to the wearer and where they don't.

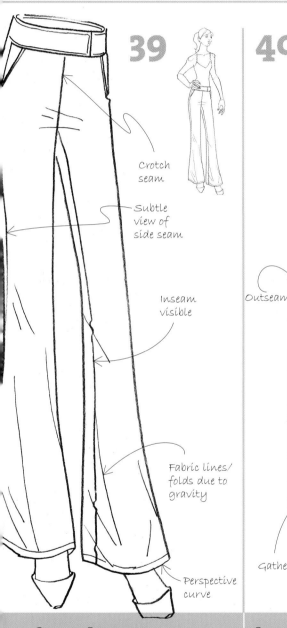

39

Crotch seam

Subtle view of side seam

Inseam visible

Fabric lines/ folds due to gravity

Perspective curve

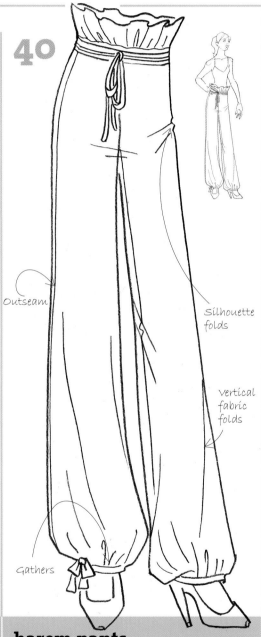

40

Outseam

Silhouette folds

Vertical fabric folds

Gathers

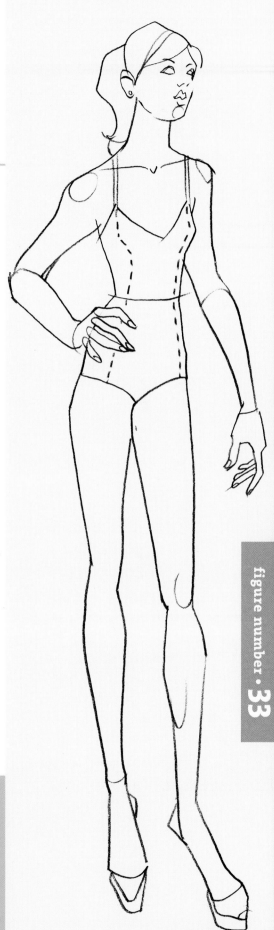

formal pants

These minimal, formal pants are designed to flatter, with subtle seaming, discreet slash pockets, and concealed "tab" closure. The cut is everything here, determining the potential leg-lengthening effect on the wearer.

harem pants

These pants are designed to be noticed, and would suit a bold fabric choice—woven or knit. Tucks and gathers take in the volume of fabric at the waist and ankle. The drawstring waist is topped by a deep, ruffled waistband, and the ankle cuffs are finished with small ribbon ties.

Pants:
Profile view

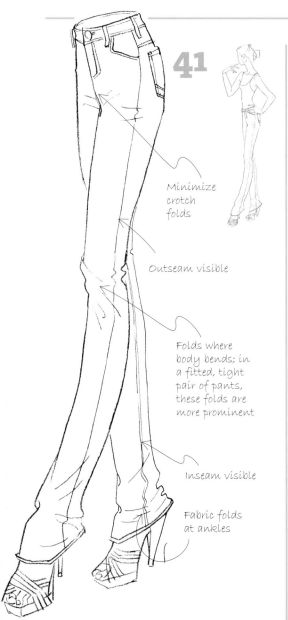

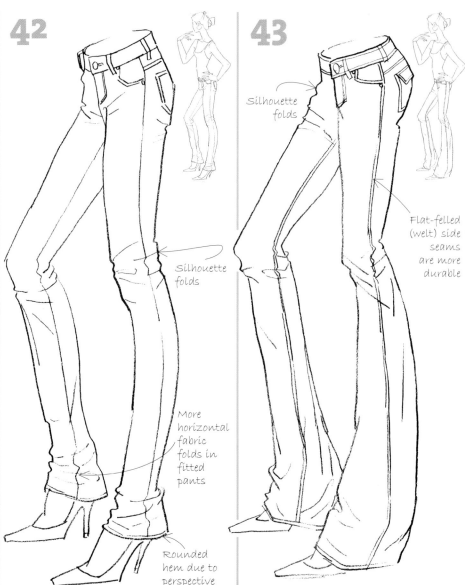

41

Minimize
crotch
folds

Outseam visible

Folds where
body bends; in
a fitted, tight
pair of pants,
these folds are
more prominent

Inseam visible

Fabric folds
at ankles

42

Silhouette
folds

More
horizontal
fabric
folds in
fitted
pants

Rounded
hem due to
perspective

43

Silhouette
folds

Flat-felled
(welt) side
seams
are more
durable

straight-leg denims

The woven fabric of these jeans hugs the wearer, thanks to a body-conscious cut and perhaps a dash of stretch in the denim. Zipper stitching, double seamlines, and pocket detailing accentuate the shape of these jeans. **Note:** Figure 32, which corresponds to this garment, can be found on page 117.

fitted jeans

These mid-rise, woven, fitted jeans fit like a second skin. Classic detailing includes zipper stitching lines, metal reinforcement rivets, and patch pockets at the back. You could add stitching detail to the pockets to personalize or brand the pants.

wide-leg jeans

These wide-leg jeans are cut with a "low-rise" waist, designed to skim the hips. At the back, flap pockets add variation to the otherwise classic denim styling of rivets and double stitching. Choose a heavyweight woven fabric for the correct drape.

Variations on pants styles are almost endless. Shown here are more formal pants and several different jeans styles displayed in a profile view. Often, subtle changes in cut or detailing can have a significant effect on the character of the finished pants and the kind of outfit they might complement.

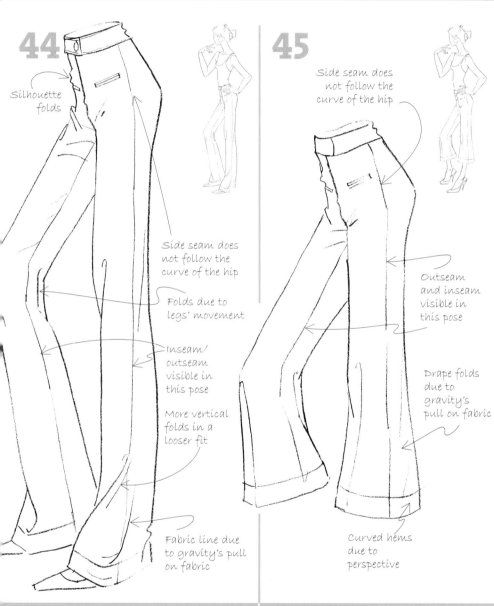

44

Silhouette folds

Side seam does not follow the curve of the hip

Folds due to legs' movement

Inseam/ outseam visible in this pose

More vertical folds in a looser fit

Fabric line due to gravity's pull on fabric

45

Side seam does not follow the curve of the hip

Outseam and inseam visible in this pose

Drape folds due to gravity's pull on fabric

Curved hems due to perspective

formal pants

These slightly looser formal pants are cut with a slight flare and turn-ups. They are high waisted, with a buttoned tab closure. A pair of double welt pockets adds detail and a high level of finish to the flat front. These pants would work in a light-to-medium-weight woven fabric.

gauchos

These cropped, wide-leg pants feature a high-tab waistband with hook closure and double welt pockets, punctuating the flat front. Note how the woven fabric drapes around the legs.

figure number • **89**

Shorts:
Length and shape

46

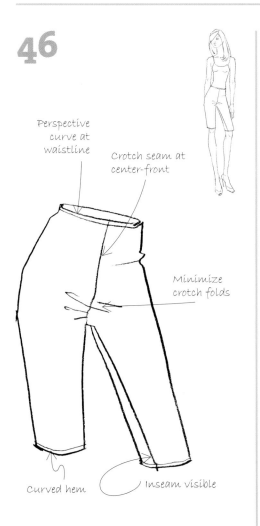

Perspective curve at waistline

Crotch seam at center-front

Minimize crotch folds

Curved hem

Inseam visible

47

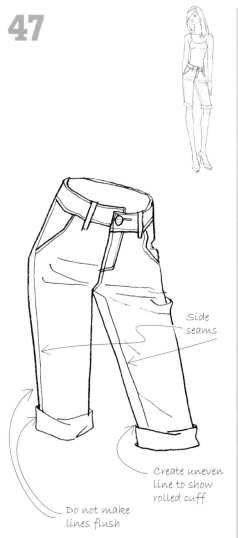

Side seams

Create uneven line to show rolled cuff

Do not make lines flush

48

Silhoue[tte] fold

Fabric folds

Curved hem

biker shorts

These close-fitting shorts may be made in woven or knit fabric. They fit the thigh and end just above the knee, with minimal seaming. This basic shorts silhouette is the block from which all other styles are adapted.

Bermuda jeans

These shorts are jeans at heart. They feature classic jeans styling: zippered fly with stitch lines, belt loops (place them equidistant to the center-front), and continental pockets. The legs are finished by rolled cuffs. This style would suit a woven fabric—denim or similar.

high-waisted culottes

These smart, little woven shorts are almost a skirt in silhouette. The high waist is fastened by a cased drawstring. The shorts flare out around the legs, with extra volume and movement added by the inverted pleats at the center-front of each leg.

Shorts can range from very brief and super casual to knee-length workwear in smart fabrics. Make the most of fun details such as pleats, gathers, cuffs, and decorative stitching to give them maximum personality.

49

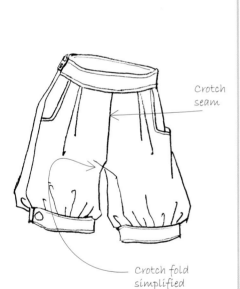

Crotch seam

Crotch fold simplified

50

Outseam

Inseam

Fabric fold due to tension created by legs' movement

figure number · 5

knickerbockers

A playful pair of shorts, with gathers at the buttoned, cuffed hemlines and tucks at the waistband. The knickerbockers are fastened by a side zipper. Try this style in either woven or knit fabric, according to your desired effect.

short denims

Like a pair of cut-off jeans, these shorts feature classic western styling: continental pockets, zipper stitch lines, a "coin" pocket, and decorative seaming. They would suit a woven fabric such as denim.

Dresses:
Short day dresses

51

Fabric folds due to hips' movement and gravity

Folds due to legs' movement

Subtle curve to hem due to angle of view

52

Uneven side line to emphasize that waistband is a separate layer

Uneven hemline to indicate opening in fabric

53

Construction folds

empire-waist dress

A simple silhouette with tasteful detailing, including covered and looped buttons, shoulder gathers, and bust darts. The cleverly cut woven fabric of this versatile favorite drapes and folds around the body, falling from a pointed empire waist.

shirtdress

A funky rendition of a classic, this shirtdress is given extra personality by way of shoulder gathers, full bishop sleeves, and a wide ribbon tie belt. It retains typical shirtdress detailing such as tailored cuffs and a center-front pleat. Here, the neckline is plain but you could add a shirt or blouse collar. This dress would work best in a woven fabric.

shirred bubble dress

Worked in a woven fabric, this bubble dress features generous shirring (rows of gathers used to add volume), falling toward an uneven, rounded hem. It is given a harder edge by a square neckline.

Short day dresses range from the simple shift and workmanlike shirt dress to more fun and sexy sundresses and halters. Experiment with sleeve lengths and other construction details, and you will find that there is a dress for every eventuality.

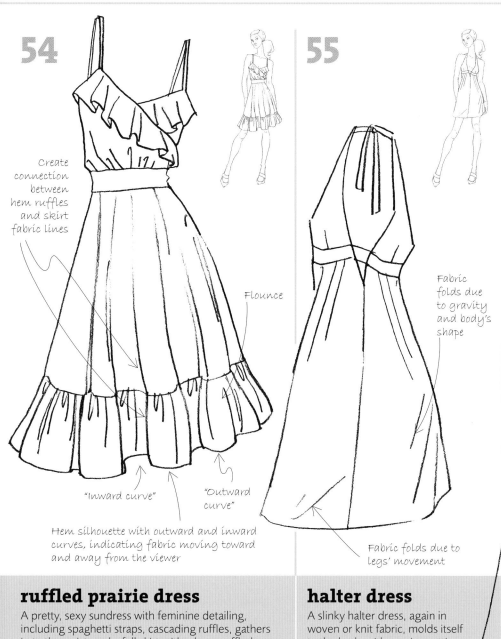

54

Create connection between hem ruffles and skirt fabric lines

Flounce

"Inward curve"

"Outward curve"

Hem silhouette with outward and inward curves, indicating fabric moving toward and away from the viewer

55

Fabric folds due to gravity and body's shape

Fabric folds due to legs' movement

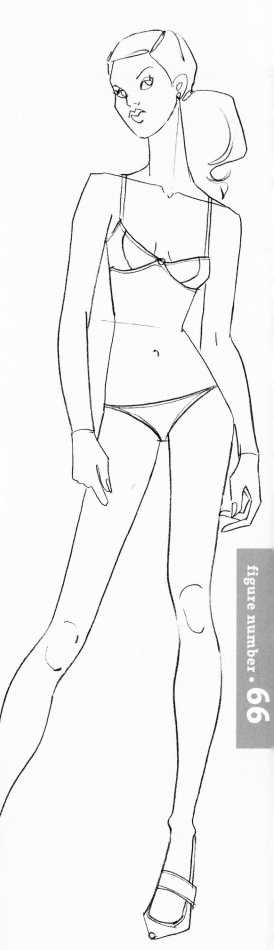

ruffled prairie dress

A pretty, sexy sundress with feminine detailing, including spaghetti straps, cascading ruffles, gathers in to the waist, and a full skirt with a large ruffled flounce. Try this dress in woven or knit fabrics for different effects—either stiffer or more draped.

halter dress

A slinky halter dress, again in woven or knit fabric, molds itself to the body with precise cutting and bust darts. A deep plunge neckline is balanced by the knee-length skirt.

Dresses:
Sleeveless day dresses

56

Silhouette
folds

Fabric folds
due to legs'
movement

Gravity folds

57

Silhouette
folds

Folds and
gathers due
to the crunch
created by
the belt

Movement
folds

58

Outward
folds

Inward
folds

Inward
curves

Outward
curves

empire-waist dress

Use knit fabric for this simple, sexy sundress.
A V-neck style with shoulder gathers; further
shape is added by bust darts. The fabric drapes
beautifully around the body from the empire
waist, falling in folds around the movement
of the legs.

layered blouson dress

Bust gathers shape the top part of this
layered summer dress; it is gathered
at the hips by a belt made of the same
fabric. The layered skirt adds movement
to the design. Use woven or knit fabric,
and try changing the length for a
different feel.

layered ruffled dress

This delicate, feminine dress would lend itself
to a light, woven fabric. A generously ruffled
skirt is gathered in to a deep waistband just
below the bust. Slender spaghetti straps finish
the design.

This selection of short day dresses demonstrates the versatility of a basic block. Use gathers, darts, and self-fabric belts to fit the dress to the body; create drama and interest with ruffles, cascades, and shirring. Play with fabrics to extend the range of possible effects.

59

Construction and drape folds

Hem ruffles created by waist gathers

Fabric folds due to legs' movement

60

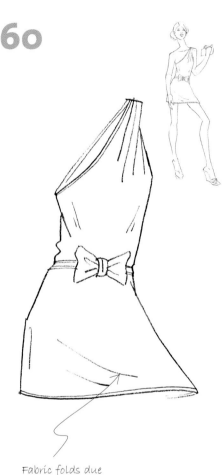

Fabric folds due to legs pulling the skirt piece

figure number • 24

strapless cascade dress

This strapless dress features shirring and cascades for a textural, sculptural effect in a woven fabric. The shirring defines the bust, then drapes in soft gathers to form the full, floaty skirt. The cascade at one side shows off the front and back of the fabric, and could be used to add a color contrast.

unishoulder minidress

This short, sassy, one-shoulder design may be made in woven or knit fabric. The dress is gathered at the shoulder and finished with a fun "bow tie" belt. You could change the length of this block for a completely different, more sophisticated effect.

Evening gowns:
Cocktail dresses

Evening dresses depend on drama, but this can come in a range of guises. Play with proportion, embellishment, fit, and flare. Always choose luxurious fabrics, though these may be woven or knit, depending on the effect you want to achieve.

61

Construction and drape folds

62

"Wrap" straps around body

Silhouette fold

Drape folds

63

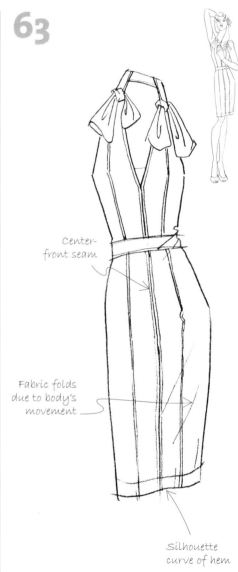

Center-front seam

Fabric folds due to body's movement

Silhouette curve of hem

panier dress

This very short, woven or knit dress is cowled to give a "sack" silhouette. A cowl is formed by anchoring fabric at two points and allowing it to drape between these fixed positions. This design is finished by a neck tie detail.

shirred minidress

This shirred minidress would work in woven or knit fabric. It has a bloused upper half, falling from neckline gathers to the dropped waist, below which the short skirt is cut close to the body.

sheath cocktail dress

This extremely fitted, woven sheath dress has piping to emphasize the structural seaming and along the waistband. Narrow halter straps are embellished with two bow ties.

64

65

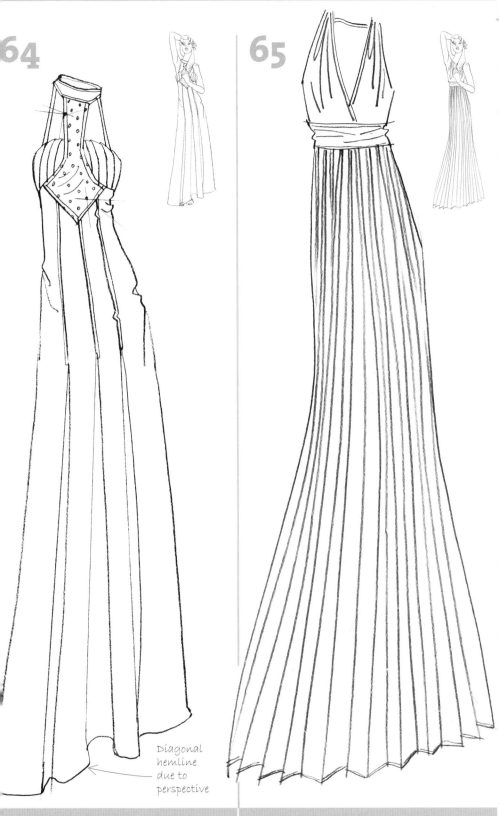

Diagonal hemline due to perspective

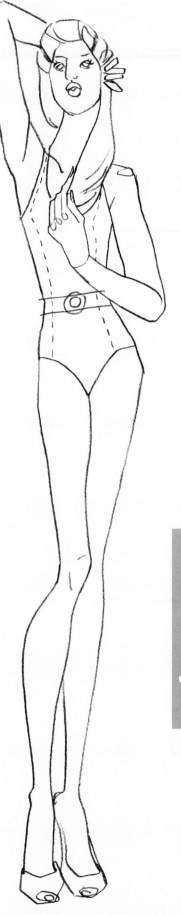

pleated dress

Use fabrics that will drape well, such as silk satin or charmeuse, for this elegant dress with three piped, inverted pleats. The bodice is fitted, with expanded tucks over the bust and a banded halter neckline with a front panel studded with rhinestones or sequins. The dress flares toward foot level thanks to the pleats, which skim the waist and hips.

accordion pleat dress

This accordion pleat dress has a full skirt of sheer, lightweight woven or knit fabric, such as georgette or chiffon. The small pleats are placed equidistant from one another along the control seam at the lower edge of the empire-waist yoke. The dress features a simple, deep, V-neckline with gathers over the bust.

Evening gowns:
Long silhouette

66

Movement folds

Drape folds due to pull of gravity on fabric

Curve the hem

67

Silhouette folds created where body bends

Movement and drape folds

Hem flare

68

Draw lines that intertwine to represent "cowled" fabric

Frontal-plane folds

Perspective curve

halter maxidress

This relaxed, empire-waist dress is designed for a soft, knit fabric, which will drape around the body. Darts below the bust reduce the fabric volume around the waist. The neckline is a simple halter.

bias-cut dress

This floor-length dress has a fitted corset bodice. Though the fabric is woven, it clings to the body because it is cut on the bias. There is a "control seam" at knee level, and below this the fabric is circular-cut for added fullness and flare.

cowl neck blouson dress

A slightly more relaxed fit is created by the draped cowl neckline and dropped waist silhouette. Fabric from the bodice is gathered into the waist wrap, and the very full skirt brushes the floor. Use a crisp fabric that will hold its shape, such as taffeta.

These dresses share a long silhouette, but use a range of finishes and construction details to create very different effects. Fabrics can vary from knit to stiffly woven for a range of occasions, from relaxed to formal.

69

Uneven line to show waistband is a separate layer of fabric

Construction/drape folds

70

Construction folds created by waist pleats

figure number • 66

layered gown

This is a variation on the pleated gown, again with a princess-seamed bodice and spaghetti straps. Here, an asymmetrical waist wrap has been added, and a flounce at mid-thigh level, below which the skirt fabric falls in soft pleats to the floor.

pleated gown

This gown creates a romantic silhouette, with its delicate spaghetti straps, princess-seamed bodice, and criss-cross waist wrap. The full skirt is gently pleated and flares dramatically toward the hemline. Use woven fabric.

Evening gowns:
Profile view

71

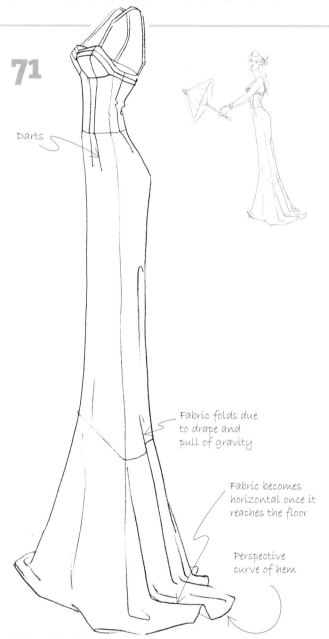

Darts

Fabric folds due
to drape and
pull of gravity

Fabric becomes
horizontal once it
reaches the floor

Perspective
curve of hem

72

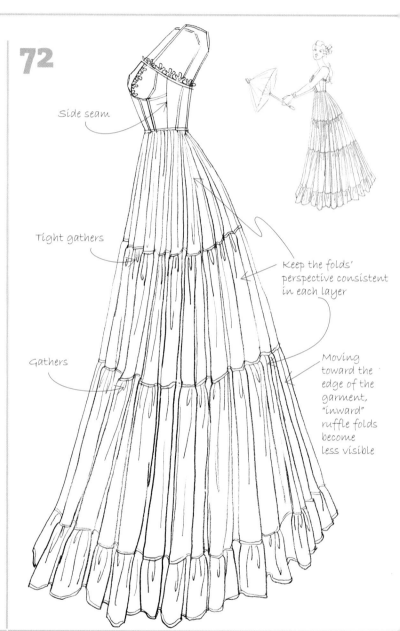

Side seam

Tight gathers

Gathers

Keep the folds'
perspective consistent
in each layer

Moving
toward the
edge of the
garment,
"inward"
ruffle folds
become
less visible

bias-cut evening gown

This extra-long, bias-cut gown has a simple bustier-style
bodice with princess seams and delicate straps. The
woven fabric of the skirt drapes beautifully around
the body, aided by both the bias cut and gravity.

Victorian tiered gown

Again, a tight, fitted, seamed bodice—here, with corset
boning to add structure. The full, tiered skirt has tight
gathers at the waist and at each tier, creating an extremely
ruffled effect at the floor-length hem. Use a luxurious
woven fabric for this dress.

Take the basic block of a tight bodice, and add different styles and lengths of skirts and other embellishments, to create all kinds of sumptuous and fanciful evening gowns. There are three versions shown here, but really, the only limit is your imagination.

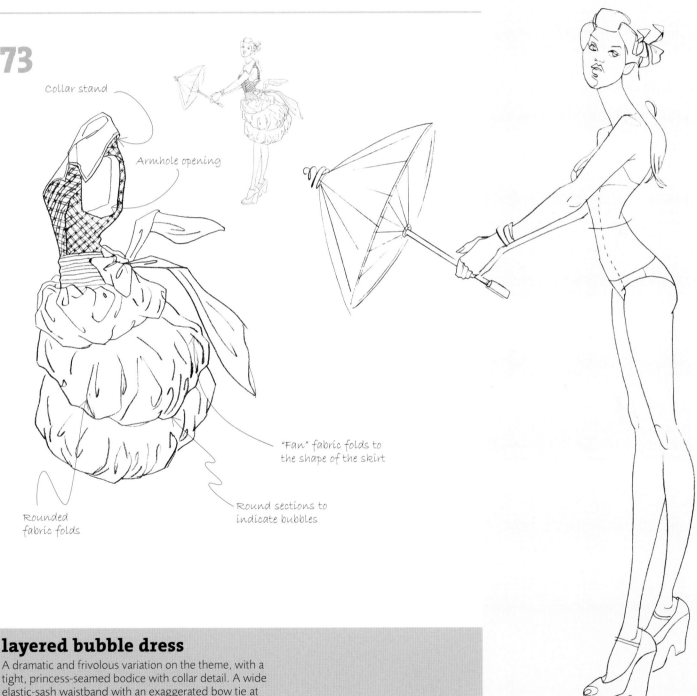

73

Collar stand

Armhole opening

"Fan" fabric folds to the shape of the skirt

Rounded fabric folds

Round sections to indicate bubbles

layered bubble dress

A dramatic and frivolous variation on the theme, with a tight, princess-seamed bodice with collar detail. A wide elastic-sash waistband with an exaggerated bow tie at the back tops a short but voluminous layered bubble skirt. The fabric of the skirt falls in layers to the knee-length hem. Again, use a woven fabric for this design.

Outerwear:
Suit jackets

74

75

Winged collar

Double breasted

Bellows pockets

variation

Welt-flap pocket

76

Movement folds at elbow

tailored vest

The basic suit bodice block includes typical tailored details such as a single-breasted, notched collar made of a top collar and lapel. The garment is fitted to the body with darts and features welt-flap pockets.

short-sleeved jacket

A variation on the basic bodice block, with short sleeves gathered into shoulder epaulettes, for a slightly military feel. The garment is fitted to the body with darts, and features welt-flap pockets. Use woven fabric.

single-breasted jacket

A classic, single-breasted jacket design with notched collar, armhole princess seams to fit the body, and buttoned cuffs. Use woven fabric; the choice of weight will greatly influence the finished effect.

These formal, masculine, structured styles of outerwear are built up from the basic block of the suit bodice. Add sleeves and collars, and vary the length to create a range of jackets for every occasion.

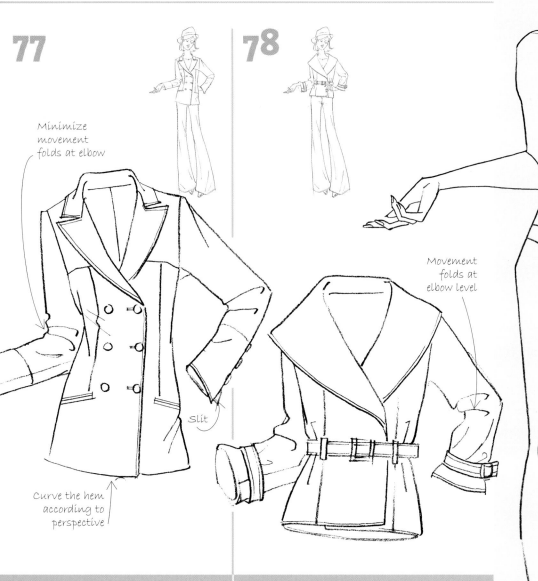

77

Minimize movement folds at elbow

Slit

Curve the hem according to perspective

78

Movement folds at elbow level

double-breasted jacket

A longer-line jacket, with double-breasted front. This design features a range of extra details: bust yoke, slit and buttoned cuffs, peaked lapels, and double-welt pockets. Place the rows of buttons equidistant from the center-front.

shawl collar belted jacket

This smoking-style jacket wraps around the body and is fastened with a buckled belt. Cuffs with buckled tabs continue the theme. A generous shawl collar provides a dramatic sweep of fabric at the neckline. Princess seams fit the jacket to the figure.

Outerwear:
Casual jackets

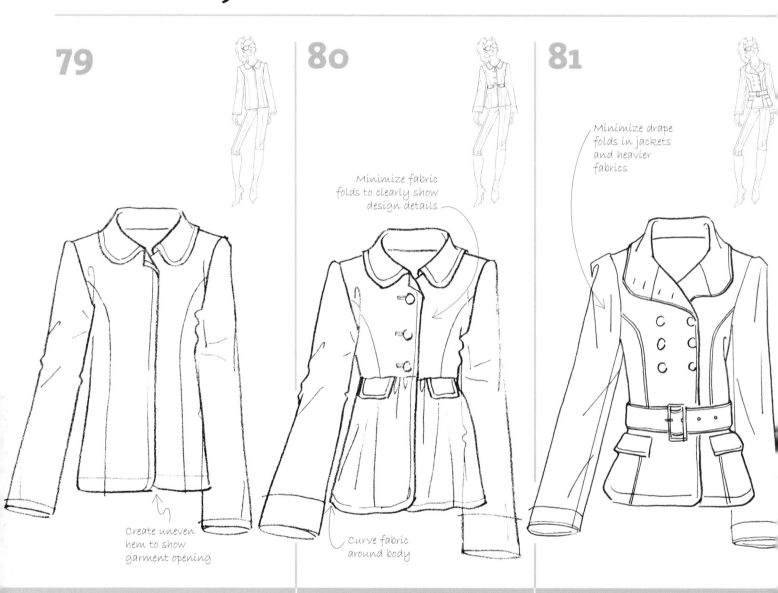

79

Create uneven hem to show garment opening

80

Minimize fabric folds to clearly show design details

Curve fabric around body

81

Minimize drape folds in jackets and heavier fabrics

basic jacket

This basic jacket would work in woven or knit fabric; the heavier the fabric, the rounder the "corners." This design features armhole princess seams and a rounded, convertible collar. The concealed, "leading-edge" opening slightly crosses the center-front line.

empire-waist jacket

Again, use woven or knit fabric for this feminine jacket. It has a rounded collar and a single-breasted opening—the buttons fall on the center-front line. The silhouette flares out slightly from the high empire waist, and is also slightly flared at the cuff.

double-breasted jacket

This jacket is designed for fairly heavy, woven fabric (heavier fabric makes for rounder "corners"). It is double-breasted—place the two lines of buttons equidistant from the center-front line. It is finished with a buckled belt and flap pockets.

A basic jacket block can be adapted in a variety of ways—change the length and opening style, add a belt, vary the collar type, or even remove the collar altogether. Note: jackets for women open with the right side overlapping the left.

82

Patch pockets

Waist darts

83

Silhouette folds

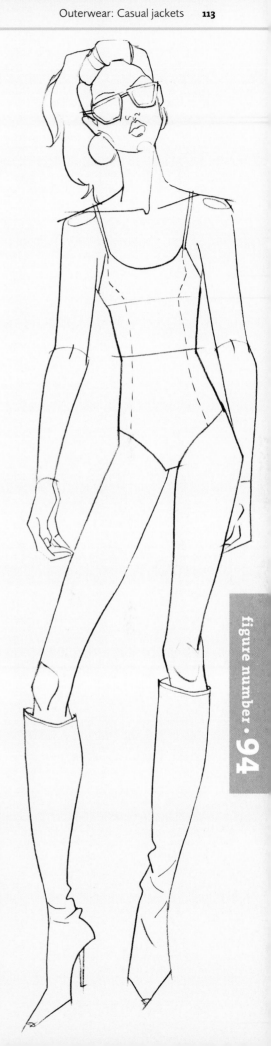

figure number • **94**

blazer

A relaxed, loose-fitting, masculine-style blazer with a single-breasted, single-button fastening. It has a notched collar (top collar and lapel), rolled cuffs, and patch pockets.

motorcycle jacket

This hard-edged jacket is designed for leather or suede (though you could use other fabrics). It is fitted close to the body with armhole princess seams, and is collarless. It has two slanted, zippered-welt pockets, buttoned cuffs, and "two-piece" sleeves.

Collars:
Three-quarter view

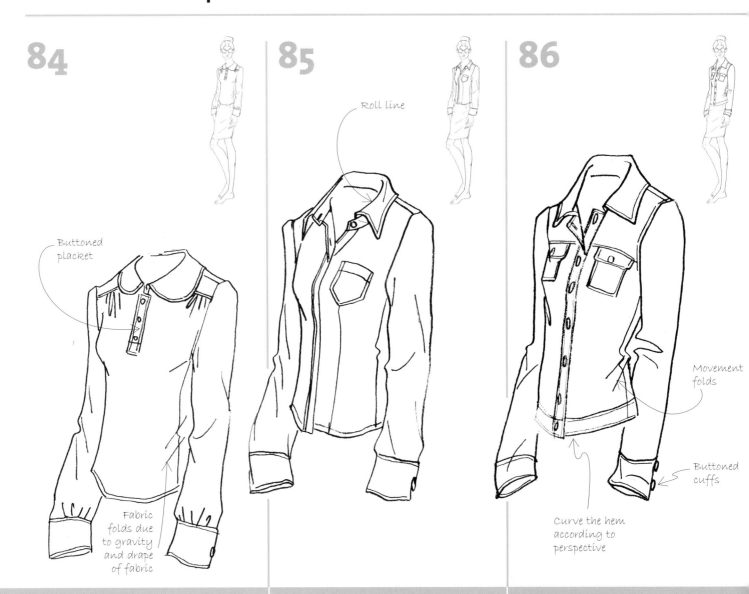

84

Buttoned placket

Fabric folds due to gravity and drape of fabric

85

Roll line

86

Movement folds

Buttoned cuffs

Curve the hem according to perspective

Peter Pan collar

This woven blouse features a Peter Pan collar, gathered shoulders, shirt cuffs, and a buttoned placket. This type of collar has no stand and a round edge for quite a feminine look.

spread or shirt collar

A fitted woven shirt with a "spread" or shirt collar, patch pocket, waist darts, and buttoned-band cuff. The classic shirt collar has a stand, giving a sharper, more masculine effect.

jacket collar: convertible

This fitted woven shirt has a convertible collar, buttoned cuffs, and two patch pockets with buttoned flaps. The collar has a stand and, when open, a small lapel.

Collars "finish" the neck openings of shirts, blouses, jackets, coats, and dresses. Crisp and sharp, or soft and rounded, your choice of collar will give the completed garment its own distinct personality.

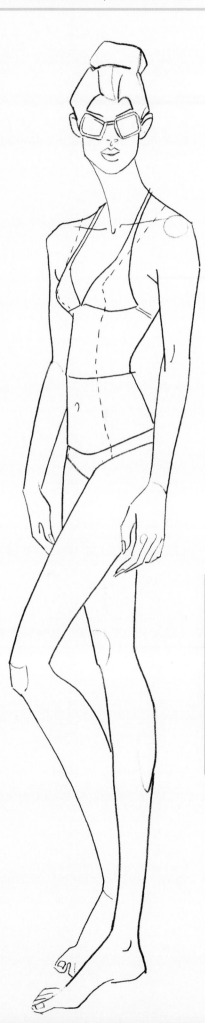

87

Buttons fall on center-front line

88

Gorge line

Top collar

Notch

Lapel

Side seam

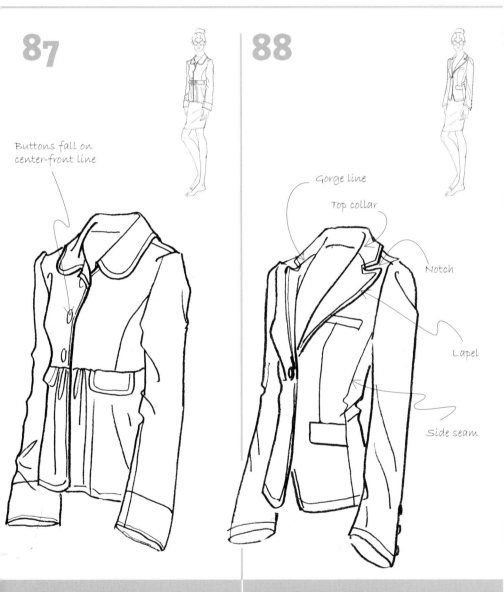

jacket collar: rounded edge

This jacket is made from heavier woven fabric than the shirts, giving it "rounder" edges and curves. It has two flap pockets at the empire waist and a rounded collar, for a soft, feminine appearance.

notched collar

This fitted jacket has a notched collar, which consists of two parts—the top collar and the lapel, divided by the notch. It is fitted to the body with darts and has three-buttoned tailored cuffs.

Footwear:
Boots and shoes

89 basic pumps

These pumps have a mid-height stiletto heel, pointed toe box, and plain vamp. They form the basis for a range of variations; some are shown here.

90 strapped pumps

Wrap the straps around the foot by curving them

Perspective curve

91 bow-tie pumps

92 peep-toe pumps

Open toe box

93 gathered peep toes

Gathered vamp

94 basic boots

These leather boots have a mid-height heel, and finish below the knee. Areas under tension will have additional layers, special finishing, piping, and stitchwork for support and reinforcement.

Side seams

Center-front line

Silhouette folds where there is a bend

Pulls

95 rounded toe cowboy boots

A few silhouette folds define the position and movement of the foot

96 pointed toe cowboy boots

Stitchwork design

The softer the boot material, the more folds and lines will be visible, but try to minimize them

shoe terminology

Insole: Inside layer of shoe.
Vamp: Upper portion of shoe. Houses a variety of design elements, such as bows, gathers, lacing, straps, and so on.
Toe box: Can take on a variety of shapes, from round, to pointed, to open (peep toe).
Outsole: Bottom portion of shoe.
Arch: The curvature of a shoe. The higher the heel, the steeper and more exaggerated the arch becomes.
Heel: A major determinant of the shoe silhouette. Can be low or high—for example, flat, stiletto, wedge, platform, etc.

Profile view

Arch

Top piece

Toe box

Outsole

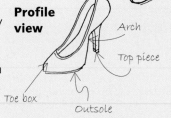

Three-quarter view

Insole

Heel

Vamp

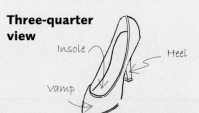

Here, four basic shoe and boot styles are adapted to form new styles. The parts of a shoe are also explained; these components can be adjusted separately to form many different variations.

97 riding boots

These soft, leather or fabric boots have a mid-height heel and are knee-length. They have zippered inseams and fit closely to the leg. They also feature straps and buckles for design and reinforcement in tension areas.

Soft leather or fabric will create more folds

98 ruched knee-high boots

Cuff

Fabric or hide folds created by ruching

All-over silhouette folds show gathers

Stiletto/ spiked heels

99 gathered ankle boots

These short, leather ankle boots have high heels and platform soles. This style also features center-front gathers.

Platform outsole

100 laced platform boots

Lacing

Zippered inseam

Silhouette folds

Perforated outsole

101 peep-toe boots

Gathers created by straps

Accessories: Bags and purses

102 clutch

This small, clutch-type purse would complement evening wear but would not be practical for everyday use. It features a clasp closure and would typically be made in a luxurious fabric and possibly embellished, as shown here.

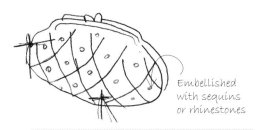

Embellished with sequins or rhinestones

105 fanny pack

This fanny pack is designed to sit on the hips of the wearer. It has a zippered opening and two front pockets. Make it in sturdy fabric or even leather.

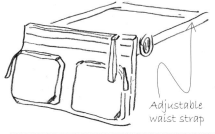

Adjustable waist strap

103 basic purse

This timeless purse design works for any occasion and would finish a range of outfits. Make it in leather for a luxury feel; choose the finish and color with care.

Straps affixed to bag by strap loops

104 purse with gathers

A variation on the basic purse theme, this gathered purse would work in a softer leather to accentuate the detailing and shape. This is a slightly dressier style that would look good with more feminine clothing.

Gathers create volume

106 striped satchel

A stylish and practical version of a larger bag, this striped satchel features shaped handles attached by rings and riveted loops. With bags, much of the drama comes from such attention to small, structural details.

Zippered pockets and opening

107 chain-strap purse

This purse is a classic twist on the basic style, with chain straps providing interest. The tabbed magnetic closure is practical, but at the same time adds a visual feature.

Side bow details

Zippered pocket

A bag or a purse is not only practical but adds the finishing touch to an outfit. The range shown here covers everything from a diminutive, sparkly evening clutch, to sumptuous leather purses with designer detailing, and larger bags designed to contain all kinds of essentials.

108 ruffled satchel

Made in soft leather, this satchel has playful detailing in the form of ruffles originating from the straps around the body of the bag.

Zippered opening

109 ostrich bag

A slouchy, single-strap shoulder bag; this would work well in a decorative, grainy leather such as ostrich, as shown here. An oversized buckle adds focus to the front.

Extend ostrich marks beyond outline to give the impression of depth

110 messenger bag

This simple bag shape lends itself to a range of treatments and fabrics and would work for many different situations. Change the details to give it personality. Here it has been given straightforward clasp openings and a chunky buckled decoration.

111 hand luggage/briefcase

This capacious carrier has an angular, masculine feel that would work in thick leather or heavyweight canvas. Note the topstitching, which adds interest and also, importantly, strength.

Buckled pockets

Structured handles

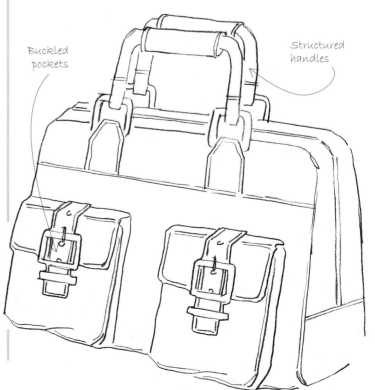

Men's garments:
Basics

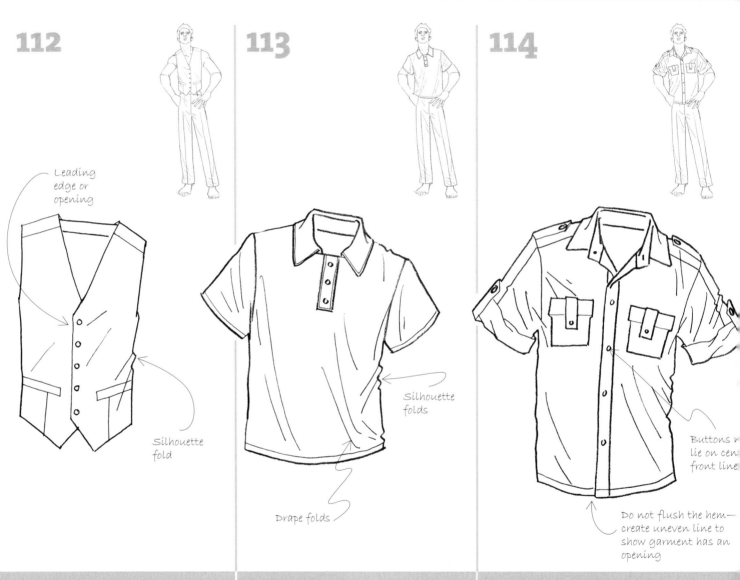

112

Leading edge or opening

Silhouette fold

113

Silhouette folds

Drape folds

114

Buttons lie on center front line

Do not flush the hem— create uneven line to show garment has an opening

tailored vest
This classic tailored vest has two welt pockets, darts to fit it to the body, and a tuxedo hem. Note that the darts are positioned differently than on the women's version (see page 41).

polo shirt
A polo shirt is a type of casual shirt that is usually made from knit fabric. It has a shirt collar and a buttoned placket.

collared shirt
This short-sleeved, collared shirt has a number of extra features, including epaulettes, rolled tab cuffs, flap breast pockets, and a convertible collar (a kind of typical shirt collar).

Here is a basic selection of men's garments. Note that for the openings of garments such as shirts, vests, jackets, and pants, the left side overlaps the right—the other way around from the openings on women's garments.

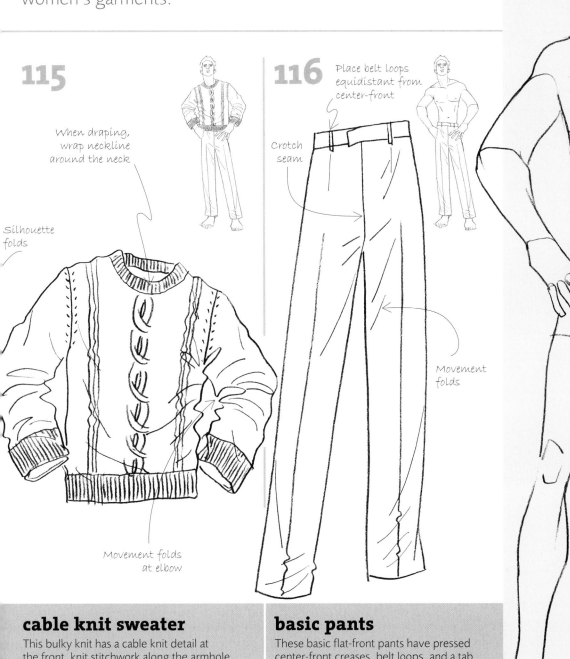

115

When draping, wrap neckline around the neck

Silhouette folds

Movement folds at elbow

116

Place belt loops equidistant from center-front

Crotch seam

Movement folds

cable knit sweater

This bulky knit has a cable knit detail at the front, knit stitchwork along the armhole seams, and deep rib knitting at the round neck, cuffs, and hem.

basic pants

These basic flat-front pants have pressed center-front creases, belt loops, and a tab waistband. Depending on the choice of fabric, they may be smart or more casual. These form the basic block for a number of pants variations and embellishments.

Clockwise from the top left:
Collection by Sylvia Kwan; figure by
the author; figure by Nanae Takata;
collection by the author.

3

Rendering techniques

In this chapter, a variety of media are used to render the draped figure.

Markers When using markers, it is advisable to render quickly, and in a circular motion in order to spread the color on the paper before it has a chance to dry and cause streaking.

Watercolor can be used for artistic or realistic rendering. When using this medium, leave areas of your canvas white. The white that peeks through will form the highlights of your illustration and is equivalent to the air in a room. You can create layered effects by applying various washes of diluted translucent watercolor to your paper, one on top of another.

Markers and watercolors each have their own advantages and appropriate usage. Markers are quick and easy to use, but you need a larger selection of colors to create your designs. Watercolor takes a bit of preparation to set up the palette and gather brushes, but with only a few colors, you can create an endless variety of tones and transparencies.

Digital rendering Use a mouse or a graphic tablet pen to paint on an electronic canvas. Although it is costlier than hand rendering, design and creative possibilities expand greatly through the use of graphic programs like Adobe Photoshop and Illustrator.

Ultimately, it's preferable to have a good base knowledge of each of the above rendering techniques and media, and to use the one that feels right and suits your specific design needs best.

1:
Leather

Leather has a smooth or grainy, slightly reflective surface and is a thick, bulky fabric. When rendering leather, it is important to add strong highlights to indicate the thick folds in the material. To do this, you could use opaque gouache or opaque white pencil.

SELECTION OF FABRIC SAMPLES

Artwork by Sylvia Kwan

Media used: Gouache, colored pencil

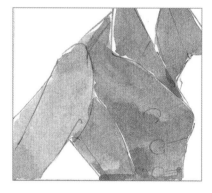

1 Apply an initial light wash as a ground color.

2 Wet-on-wet, apply a darker opaque wash on top of shadowed areas, leaving some parts exposed.

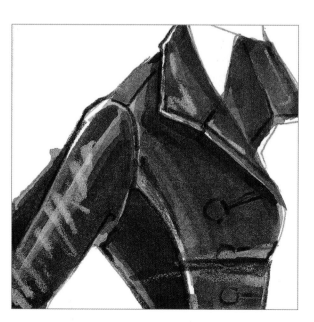

3 Once the second wash is dry, add a darker color to areas where the material overlaps. Add highlights to the folds of the garment with a white pencil.

2:
PVC

Reflective surfaces show a greater range of values. Apply a light wash first, but leave a thin shape of highlight that will run along the side of your form. This shape will "spare out" the white on your illustration. Apply further, darker washes, and then take a white pencil and define the highlights.

SELECTION OF FABRIC SAMPLES

Artwork by Sylvia Kwan

Media used: Gouache, colored pencil

2 Reapply the next layer, wet-into-wet, with a slightly darker wash as the "medium"-level shadow.

1 Apply a light wash as a ground color, leaving some areas of the paper white.

3 Using a more opaque color, paint the next layer onto selected areas of shadow.

4 For the final layer, apply a thick layer of opaque color on top of pure solid shadows that have no reflection. Take a white pencil and redefine details of drapery and seams, or any areas that reflect light.

3:

Lace

Lace will show transparent effects, so you will need to draw the base color of the form under the lace. Think about this color: if you see a body color under the lace, use a flesh-toned layer on the first color gradation. Determine the lace pattern and draw it in. Use a thick brush to create the rough texture of lace. To get form and dimension into your illustration, draw in the light and dark values.

Artwork by Nanae Takata

SELECTION OF FABRIC SAMPLES

Media used: Pencil, gouache paint, white pencil

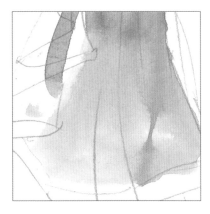

1 Pencil in the shape. Indicate folds and details. Fill in the underneath layer with a light wash.

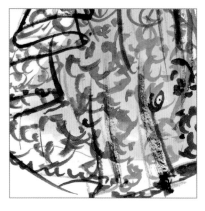

2 Cover the entire area with the lace pattern. Outline the shape with the same line quality.

3 Using a thicker brush, dry-brush (lay down thick paint with a dry brush to create this hairy texture) over the entire area. Lay down another layer in the shadow areas. Add lights with the white pencil.

4: Sheer fabric

Many fabrics have a transparent effect, meaning that you can see through them. Draw these by completing the background color first and then applying the transparent layer over it. Chiffon, tulle, and lace are examples of fabrics that are sheer. Create a wash over the shape of the fabric after applying the background color. In areas that don't cover the body, use a light-value wash.

SELECTION OF FABRIC SAMPLES

Artwork by Nanae Takata

Use darker washes for overlapping folds. The transparent fabric often covers another fabric. In this case, the value will be affected by the color and value of the overlapping sheer fabric. Each medium is slightly different in approach, but all techniques demand the application of layers.

Media used: Pencil, gouache paint

1 Fill in the skin tone (or the color of whatever garment shows through the sheer outer layer). The part that shows through should be colored using the same colored paint, but diluted. Let it dry completely.

2 With sheer fabrics, the key is to be very quick. Do not worry about filling in every corner with the color. Let the paintbrush, full of watered-down paint, "flow" over the shape in the direction of the drape. Apply a second coat to indicate shadow. Complete by reinforcing the outlines with pencil.

5:

Cotton print

When a print crosses a fold it will not join seamlessly into the next area of fabric. Use this to give your printed garment three-dimensionality. And use weighted line quality to indicate the texture of a crisp, clean fabric, such as cotton, beneath the print.

Artwork by Sylvia Kwan

SELECTION OF FABRIC SAMPLES

Media used: Watercolor, pencil, colored pencil

1 Apply the first layer of ground color.

2 After the first layer is dry, reapply the same color on areas of shadow. (There is only one layer of shadow.)

3 Add opaque layers of paint to the area of the print, blocking in the general shapes of the print.

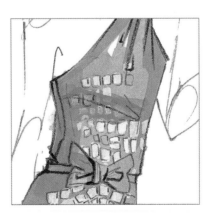

4 Add a second layer to the printed area. Take a pencil and redefine the shapes of the pattern. With a black pencil, use weighted lines to contour the crispness of the cotton fabric.

6:
Animal print

Complicated prints, such as animal prints, may be drawn in their entirety, or you can simply select certain areas of the garment to fill with print to give an impression of the pattern, leaving the rest of the garment blank.

SELECTION OF FABRIC SAMPLES

Artwork by Sylvia Kwan

Media used: Gouache, colored pencil, pencil

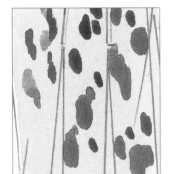

1 Apply the ground color of the fabric with a wash. Paint in the main shapes of the print only on selected areas.

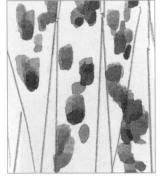

2 Taking the second print color, apply another layer of print shapes over the top of the first print shapes.

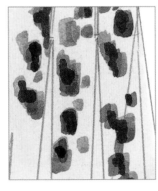

3 Using a darker, more opaque color, paint further print shapes over selected areas that you want to define.

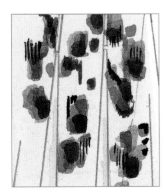

4 With the same color, add parallel line texture to indicate the direction of the print.

5 Continue to apply the parallel line texture with a pencil. Use the pencil to create areas of shadow in the fabric.

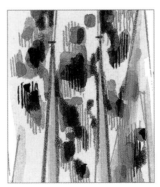

6 Apply a darker version of the ground color to the shadowed areas of the garment (in pleats etc.). Using a colored pencil, define seam detailing and add further detail to the animal print shapes.

7:
Corduroy

Cord does not reflect a lot of light; it is dull like velvet, and therefore requires softly blended areas of light and dark to demonstrate this. Concentrate on creating the highly textured lined surface of cord, which should follow the contours of the body beneath.

Artwork by Nanae Takata

SELECTION OF FABRIC SAMPLES

Media used: Pencil, colored pencil, gouache paint

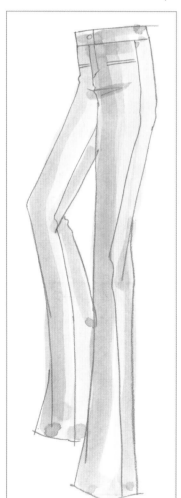 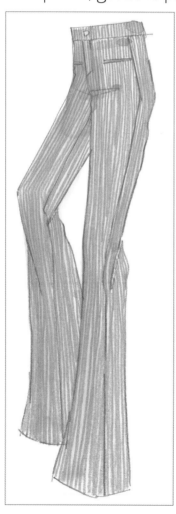 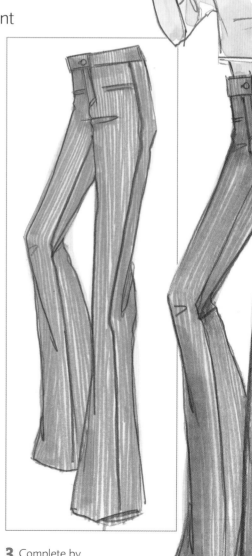

1 Apply a wash over the entire shape. Add a second coat to indicate the shadows.

2 Fill the entire shape with vertical lines of corduroy using the appropriate colored pencil. Pay attention to the lines of the body beneath.

3 Complete by reinforcing the outlines with pencil.

8:
Denim

Denim is a rough-textured fabric. Think about its weight and texture when you illustrate it. Denim comes in a variety of colors, so create a color swatch before working directly on the illustration.

SELECTION OF FABRIC SAMPLES

Artwork by Nanae Takata

Media used: Pencil, marker, colored pencils

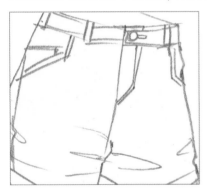

1 Pencil in all details and folds.

2 Fill in the solid areas with an appropriate colored marker, leaving the seams white.

3 Run the fine point of the white pencil diagonally to indicate the twill weave. Rub with the white pencil wherever the denim is faded. This step is very important in showing the casual and rough characteristics of denim.

4 Add in stitches and details with the appropriate colored pencils. Complete by reinforcing the outlines with pencil.

9:
Knitted

Knitwear is interesting both in silhouette and texture. There is a wide variety of complexity of knits—some can look almost sculptural. Experiment with covering the entire illustration with the stitch texture, or try a more minimal approach by drawing the stitches in areas where light and shadow meet.

Artwork by Sylvia Kwan

SELECTION OF FABRIC SAMPLES

Media used: Gouache, colored pencil

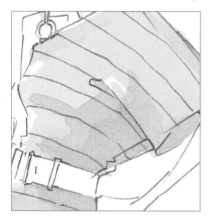

1 Apply a light wash of the fabric ground color. Once the first wash is dry, reapply on any large areas of shadow.

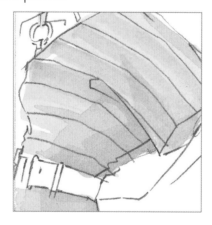

2 Paint lightly over each individual stripe with the ground color wash. Paint loosely, not filling the shape completely.

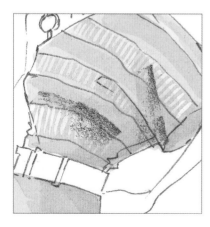

3 Add the texture of the ribbed knitwear with opaque white paint. Indicate fold lines and shadows by using swift strokes of a pencil on its side. This will give more weight to the knit.

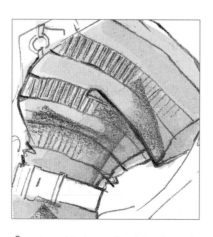

4 Using a black pencil, add weighted lines to the garment to define a selected area of the ribbing. Weighted lines should be slightly uneven to mimic the surface of knit.

10:
Stretch sports

Keep it simple when rendering this smooth, matte fabric. Use only a minimal amount of paint tones (just two or three) in the illustration to depict the finely woven surface texture of the fabric.

SELECTION OF FABRIC SAMPLES

  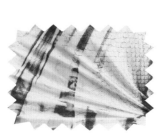

Artwork by Sylvia Kwan

Media used: Gouache, colored pencil

1 Paint a wash of the fabric ground color all over the garment, leaving areas of white paper exposed.

2 Once the first wash is dry, use the same color to add shading to overlapping and gathered areas of the fabric.

3 Add darker tones to shadowed areas to define shapes.

4 Only two tones of paint are used for stretch sportswear.

11:
Sequins

You can create sparkle fabric textures by working on a toned surface. Concentrate on the light areas of the garment by first applying the lightest areas of color, then roughly indicate the sequins over the entire surface area, with more detail on the lighter spots. Look for the light source and add a sparkle on the garment closest to this. Star-shaped lines can be used to indicate a sparkle.

SELECTION OF FABRIC SAMPLES

Artwork by Nanae Takata

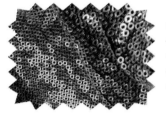  

Media used: Pencil, oil pastel, white-out

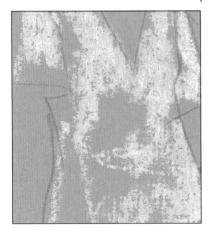

1 When working with oil pastels to illustrate light-colored garments, you should ideally work on a darker surface. Here, a medium-gray pastel paper is used. Start by roughly indicating the light areas with the appropriate color.

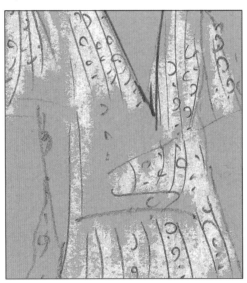

2 Add details of sequins roughly over the entire area.

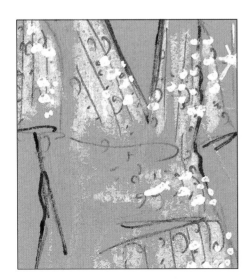

3 Add the lightest lights with the white-out. Add the sparkle at the point closest to the light to indicate shine.

12:
Stripes

It is important that a patterned fabric, such as one with stripes, follows the contours of the body. Use areas where the stripe curves under and reappears to show that there is a fold or a contour in the fabric, to give a three-dimensional quality.

SELECTION OF FABRIC SAMPLES

Artwork by Nanae Takata

Media used: Pencil, marker

1 Pencil in the stripes lightly. The stripes should follow the lines of the body.

2 Fill in the stripes with an appropriate colored marker.

3 Add the shadows. Complete the drawing by reinforcing the folds and outlines with pencil.

13:
Faux fur

Fur is a softly textured fabric that you can render by blending washes of gouache. Use two values and wet-into-wet techniques with watercolor application. Fur must be drawn to show its character, whether the hair is long, short, or curled. Add pencil lines over the wash as a second layer. The contour outlines of fur should be non-enclosed outlines that illustrate the individual hairs. Fur garments are heavy, and they drape with thick folds.

SELECTION OF FABRIC SAMPLES

Artwork by Sylvia Kwan

Media used: Watercolor, gouache, colored pencil

1 Paint a light wash of the ground color. Apply a darker layer for areas that are darker.

2 After the first layer is dry, paint another layer of darker color on top of the mid-tone areas of the fur.

3 Using the "wet-into-wet" technique, apply another layer of the ground color.

4 After the garment is completely dry, take opaque black paint and selectively choose areas that are the darkest part of the fur. Redefine the fur texture with a colored pencil.

5 Add additional texture and detail to the hair of the fur with black and white pencils. Taking the black pencil, add weighted uneven lines to indicate the thickness of the fur fabric.

14: Tweed jacket

Rough-textured fabrics can be rendered by applying gouache over a layer of watercolor. Allow a little white paper to show through to keep the illustration fresh and vibrant. Notice that there are scattered flecks of color over a tweed fabric surface. Add these by dotting the gouache paint on.

SELECTION OF FABRIC SAMPLES

 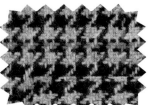 

Artwork by Sylvia Kwan

Media used: Watercolor, gouache

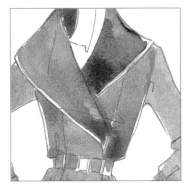

1 First, apply light wash of ground color.

2 Apply a darker layer of color, wet-into-wet, as the first layer is still wet.

3 After the second layer is dry, apply a more opaque layer of paint to shadow areas in large-shape areas.

4 Using thinner paint, add texture to the fabric by dotting the paint. Reapply to the desired areas (where the textured lines appear).

5 Reapply this technique using the opaque ground color. After this layer is dry, add black pencil to the shadow areas (use the side of the colored pencil), to add more texture.

15:
Silk satin

Shiny fabrics reflect the light. Determine where the light source is coming from, and see the highlight and shadow shapes. Look for reflected light in the shadow area. Reflected satin has similar characteristics to leather, but satin will show thinner fold widths.

SELECTION OF FABRIC SAMPLES

Artwork by Nanae Takata

Media used: Pencil, marker, white pencil

1 Pencil in all folds and details. Fill in with mid-ground tone, leaving the light areas white.

2 Fill in the white areas with white pencil. Don't hesitate to go outside the white areas. Going a little over the colored areas will create a better effect.

3 Go over the colored areas in step 2 with the same marker as you used in step 1.

4 Emphasize the lightest lights with the white pencil. Add shadows with a gray marker (20 percent gray is suggested here for light-to-medium colors, 30 percent gray is suggested for darker colors). Complete by reinforcing the outlines and folds with a pencil.

16:
Velvet

Velvet reflects very little light, and this means that your illustration will contain a minimal number of values, and the edges where light and shadow meet should be soft. This will give you a blurred look. Apply light and dark pastel or colored pencils for richness of texture. The pencil texture provides a way to blend the colors from the first layer together and bring out the soft gradations.

SELECTION OF FABRIC SAMPLES

Artwork by Nanae Takata

Media used: Pencil, pastel

1 Pencil in all details with a fairly strong line quality.

2 Fill in with the appropriate colored pastel, leaving the lights white.

3 Smear with your fingertip to fill the entire shape.

4 Add in shadows with a darker shade. Smear as needed. Complete by reinforcing the outlines with pencil.

Digital rendering

Converting a pixel drawing to a vector drawing using Adobe Illustrator

In order to be able to manipulate your scanned line drawings in digital art programs such as Illustrator, you'll need to convert them from pixel drawings to vector drawings. One of the advantages of doing this is that a vector drawing can be blown up without losing quality. Below are two methods for making this conversion.

Option 1

Make sure your original drawing is clear and the lines legible. It's best to have traced your line drawing with a pen before scanning.

1 Using the "selection" tool, select the original line drawing.

2 In the menu bar, go to "object" and select "live trace."

3 Within the live trace box, place a check next to "preview" and next to "strokes."

4 Play with the variables in the live trace box until you are satisfied with the drawing.

5 In order to make your vector drawing editable in Illustrator, using the "selection" tool, select your vector drawing. In the menu bar, under "object" select "expand." Place a checkmark next to both "fill" and "stroke." Now you can edit your lines using the "direct selection" tool.

Note: Digital rendering will be faster if all of your vector-drawing lines are closed, meaning there are no gaps in the outlines. This makes it easier to fill an area with a color or texture.

Line (pixel drawing) ⟶ 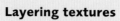 Vector drawing

Layering textures

Digital rendering allows you to experiment easily with using a combination of fabrics and textures layered together to produce a graphic illustration style.

A different look

Since each garment piece contains its own layer, you can manipulate and modify them individually to create different versions of your illustration. Here, the vest, skirt, and blouse textiles, and the ostrich leather color, have been modified for a different look.

Option 2

This option works best using a graphic pen and tablet.

1 Place your line drawing in a separate layer and lock it.

2 Create another layer. In the menu bar under "window" select "layers." You can reduce the opacity of your original drawing for better visibility of the traced drawing version.

3 Working in the newly created layer, trace your original drawing using the pen or pencil tool.

A combination of fabrics is used for textural variety here. The shirt is layered with a vest to add dimension; the plaid (gleinplaid), pinstripes, and horizontal stripes are kept flat for a graphic decorative style; and the accessories are rendered in ostrich leather.

Rendering the vest using the "pattern stamp" tool

1 The draped figure is drawn directly in Adobe Illustrator using pen and pencil tools.

2 Scan and save the desired fabric. You can manipulate the size of the plaid by changing your fabric size before defining it as a pattern.

3 Define the fabric as "pattern." In the menu bar, under "edit" choose "define pattern" and name your pattern.

4 Open your draped figure file and lock its layer. Have the layers palette open so that you have quick access to each layer. To open any palette, go to "windows" in the menu bar, and check the palette you need, in this case, the "layer" palette.

5 Select the desired garment piece using the "magic wand" or "lasso" tool from the toolbox. Create a new layer and name it, "vest fabric." To create a layer: in the menu bar, under "layer," select "new" and "layer," or click the "new layer" button at the bottom of the layers palette. It's important that you create a separate layer for each article of clothing or body area you render.

6 Choose the "pattern stamp" tool from the toolbox and in the "options bar" click "pattern picker." Find the fabric that was defined as a pattern earlier and select "vest fabric" as your active layer. Render the vest using the "pattern stamp" tool. If your outline is covered by the fabric and no longer visible, you can reduce the size of the layer containing the fabric or you can change the layer's blend mode to "multiply." Select the layer to modify, and in menu bar, under "edit" select "free transform" to reduce size manually, or select "transform" then "scale" for numeric transformation. In the options bar, you will be able to enter a numeric (percentage reduction) value for height (H) and width (W). Alternatively, to change the layer's mode to multiply: select the layer containing the fabric or skin tone. In "option bar," next to "mode" choose "multiply."

Rendering the skirt using the canvas method

1 Scan and save the desired fabric. Here, the pinstripe fabric is scanned and placed in the canvas area. Under "file" choose "place" and find your fabric.

2 Make sure the figure has its own separate layer and lock the layer.

3 Select the draped figure layer. Choose the skirt surface using the "magic wand" or "lasso" tool.

4 Place the scanned fabric into the skirt area using the "move" tool. Rotate so that the stripes are angled in the same direction as the skirt. Delete any areas of fabric that fall outside the skirt outline. **Note:** To delete excess fabric, you must "rasterize" its layer. To rasterize a layer, click the selected layer and choose "rasterize layer."

5 Adjust the color and values of the pinstripe fabric. To do this, select "image" in the menu bar and choose "adjustment" and play with the variables to achieve the desired effect.

Rendering the collared blouse

Select the layer containing the draped figure line drawing. Choose the areas of the blouse you want to render and create a new layer for rendering the blouse. Within this layer, render the blouse, using one of the methods shown on page 141. Either place the fabric directly on the canvas and "fit" it into the garment, or use the "pattern stamp" tool and render the selected areas.

Rendering the shadows

Brush strokes were added under the collar and vest for added three-dimensionality and to separate the vest layer from the shirt layer.

1 Choose the "brush" tool in the options bar, and adjust the opacity so that a transparent color is created.

2 Create a layer for rendering shadows so that you can further adjust the transparency of the shadows.

3 Select "shadow layer" as your active layer and render the shadows under the collar and around the vest using the "brush" tool.

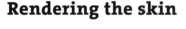

Rendering the skin

1 Choosing the draped figure as your active layer, select the areas of skin and create a new layer for the skin.

2 Set the "foreground color" (located in "toolbox") to your desired skin tone. Select the "paint bucket" tool and render the skin.

3 To create highlights, reduce the size of your "skin" layer (see step 6, "Rendering the vest," on page 141) so that the white of the canvas peeks through.

4 To create a more transparent skin tone, select the skin color layer and adjust its opacity below 100 percent.

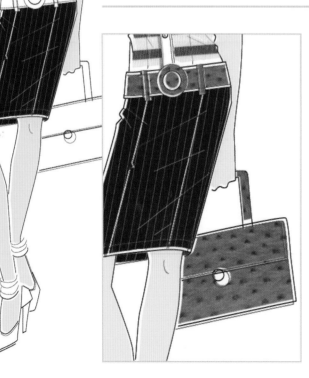

Rendering the accessories

The belt, watch, and bag were all rendered using an ostrich leather texture. To render the accessories, the "pattern stamp" method is used.

1 Define ostrich leather as a "pattern."

2 Select the draped figure layer.

3 Select the areas you want to render.

4 Create a new layer for "accessory rendering."

5 Render using the "pattern stamp" tool.

Note: By the end of your illustration, you may have many layers, and it can be time-consuming trying to find each to edit. A quick way to find and access a specific layer is to "right click ctrl+alt+click" (for PCs), or "ctrl+option+click" (for Macs) on the desired section of the canvas area. You will be taken directly to that layer.

Index

A
A-line skirts 90, 91
accessories 79, 116–117, 118–119
action lines 11
Adobe Illustrator 13, 140, 141
Adobe Photoshop 13
angle lines 11
animal print 129
apex 11

B
back view 43
    hip tilted 25
bags 118–119
balance line 11
banded-collar blouse 82
batwing dolman sleeves 88
Bermuda jeans 98
bias-cut dresses 106, 108
biker shorts 98
bikini 69
blazer 113
blouson dress 102
boots 116–117
bubble dress 109
bubble sleeves 87
    bubble-sleeve top and red
        miniskirt 21
business wear 18
    professional 40–41
    suit 36–37
    young professional 38–39
bustiers 80

C
cable knit sweater 120
cape sleeves 89
    cape-sleeve top and fitted
        denim 27
cape-collar top 81
cascades 12
    cascaded pencil skirt 90
    strapless cascade dress 103
CD 8
cigarette riding pants 94
circle sleeves with gathers 87
closures 12
collars 81, 82, 111
    collared shirt 120
    convertible 114
    three-quarter view 114–115
corduroy 130
cotton print 128
cowls 12
    cowl neck blouson dress 106
    cowl sleeves 89
creating a collection 9
culottes, high-waisted 98

D
darts 12
denim 131
    denim jacket and tiered skirt 57

denim skirt 91
    fitted denims 96
    short denims 99
design elements 12, 79
digital rendering 123, 140–142
digital tools 13
double-breasted jackets 111, 112
draping guideline 11
drawing materials 13
Drawplus 13
dresses 18
    career dresses 46–47
    casual dresses 42–43
    clubwear 50–51
    cocktail dresses 48–49, 104–105
    day dresses 44–45
    day dresses, short 100–101
    day dresses, sleeveless 102–103
    slip dress 52–53

E
ease 12
empire-waist dresses 100, 102
empire-waist jacket 112
evening wear 19
    bridal dress 62–63
    cocktail dresses 104–105
    evening dress 61
    evening gown with flounce 65
    formal/semiformal 66–67
    long silhouette 106–107
    profile view 108–109
    prom fantasy 60–61
    special occasion 64–65

F
fabric 11, 79
    folds and lines 11
    rendering techniques 124–139
fasteners 12
faux fur 136
figures 8–9, 10, 11
    dynamic figures 7, 10, 11, 15
fitted bodice with bust gathers 84
fitted skirts 90, 92
flounces 12
    evening gown with flounce 65
footwear 116–117
formal pants 95, 97
front view 60, 63
    arm lifted 35
    arms behind 26
    arms lifted 33
    crossed arms 31
    crunched 66
    figure lying with legs overlapping
        49
    hand gestures 30
    hands clasped 26
    head tilted 27
    leaning back 37
    mid-motion 50
    shifted left 56

sitting pose 77
    twisted 46
    walking 34
front view, dynamic 36, 46, 49, 50, 51,
    58, 63
    exaggerated 57
    outerwear 54, 55, 56, 57
    sportswear 26, 28, 29, 30, 34, 73
full back view 22, 34, 45, 52, 69, 71
full front view 36, 40, 42, 44, 66,
    74, 76
    arm extended 43
    dynamic 20, 40, 42, 58
    expressive 41
    hands on waist 20
    relaxed 21, 23
    sportswear 20, 23, 31, 32, 72
    static 35, 37
    subtle hip movement 22
    with profile face 44
garment blocks 7, 79
garment categories 16–19
garment construction 11
gathers 12, 84–85, 87
gauchos 97
godet skirt 91
gores 12

H
halter dress 101
halter maxidress 45, 106
harem pants 95
high hip 11

J
jackets 110–111, 112–113, 114–115
jeans
    bell-bottom 94
    Bermuda jeans 98
    fitted 94, 96
    wide-leg 96

K
kimono sleeve top and denim
    shorts 31
kimono sleeves 88
knickerbockers 99
knit fitted top 82
knitted fabrics 132

L
lace 126
    lace and plaid 29
layered dress-coat over pants 23
layered dresses 102, 107, 108
layered skirts 93
leading edge 12
leather 124
lingerie 19
    casual 68–69
    luxury 70–71
long, draping silk-satin dress 49

M
markers 13, 123
market categories 16
    markets within sportswear 17–18
media 13
menswear 19
    basics 120–121
    casual/sportswear 76–77
    classic 74–75
motorcycle jacket 113
movement 11

N
notched collar 115

O
openings 12
outerwear 18
    casual jackets 112–113
    coats and capes 58–59
    contemporary/junior 54–55
    designer outerwear 56–57
    suit jackets 110–111
overlap lines 11

P
panier dress 104
pants 120
    front view 94–95
    profile view 96–97
papers 13
peasant top 83
    peasant top with bishop sleeves 25
Peter Pan collar 114
pintucks 81
play leg 11
pleats 12
    pleated dresses 105, 107
    pleated sleeves with rib
        knitting 86
polo shirt 120
portfolios 13
profile view 36, 38, 58, 64, 74
    arms forward 65
    arms wrapped 69
    bent pose 72
    dresses 42, 46, 48, 52, 62
    leg lifted 62
    shoulders back 39
    sportswear 22, 29, 35, 54, 55, 72
    tilting back 59
    twisted 25
    upper body twisting toward the
        viewer 77
puff sleeves 86
purses 118–119
PVC 125

R
raglan sleeves 88
rendering techniques 7, 123
    digital rendering 123, 140–142
    rendering a figure 8–9

rounded edge collar 115
ruching 12
ruffles 12
   layered ruffled dress 102
   ruffled prairie dress 101
   ruffled top 80
   strapless ruffled top 85

S
sequins 134
   sequined sheath dress 51
sewing guideline 11
shape 11
shawl collar belted jacket 111
sheath dresses 51, 104
sheer fabric 127
shirring 12
   shirred bubble dress 100
   shirred minidress 104
   shirred top 85
shirt collar 114
shirtdress 47, 100
shirts 120
shoes 116–117
short-sleeved jacket 110
shorts 98–99
silhouette 11, 106–107
silk satin 138
single-breasted jacket 110
skirts
   fitted and A-line skirts 90–91
   longer and ruffled skirts 92–93
sleeves
   all-in-one sleeves 88–89
   butterfly sleeves 81
   short sleeves 86–87
slip dress 53
smocking 12
   smocked top 84
software 13
sportswear 16–17
   active sportswear 19, 72–73
   better/bridge sportswear 24–25
   contemporary 26–29
   designer sportswear 20–23
   fitness 72–73
   junior 30–31
   markets within sportswear 17–18
   missy 32–33
   women, plus-size sportswear
      34–35
spread collar 114
strap gathers 84
strapless cascade dress 103
strapless ruffled top 85
stretch sports fabrics 133
stripes 135
support leg 11
swimwear 19
   casual 68–69
   luxury 70–71

T
tailored jacket 37
tailored vests 110, 120
terminology 10–12, 116
textiles see fabric
three-quarter back view 21, 33,
   38, 48, 67

three-quarter front view 48, 50,
   52, 56, 60, 62, 68, 74
   arm lifted 38
   arms lifted 71
   assertive 39
   bending 51
   dynamic 28, 32, 55
   dynamic arms 68
   head up 75
   lifted arm 75
   reclining 61
   relaxed 75
   sitting 61, 70
   sportswear 20, 24, 32, 33, 73
   turning away 68
   walking 39
   with attitude 24
   with profile of face 76
three-quarter view 40, 44, 47, 66
   arm lifted 27, 41
   arms behind the back 45
   bending 63
   dynamic 30, 70
   dynamic exaggerated 70
   legs 59
   sitting 28, 47, 53, 67
   sitting, profile face 64
   twisted 33
tiered skirts 57, 92
tools 13
tops
   fitted 80–81
   knits and woven tops 82–83
   tops with gathers 84–85
tucks 12
tweed jacket 137

U
unishoulder minidress 103
unishoulder tunic 83

V
velvet 139
vests 110, 120
   vest, shirt and princess-seam
      skirt 41
Victorian tiered gown 108
vintage smocking 12

W
watercolor 13, 123
working by hand 8
woven fitted top 82
wrap skirt 92

Y
yokes 12

Z
zebra-print dress 43

Credits

Quarto would like to thank the following artists—who are acknowledged beside their work—for kindly supplying images for inclusion in this book:

Sylvia Kwan was born and raised in Pennsylvania and is a graduate of Parsons the New School for Design in New York. Sylvia currently lives and works in New York City.

Nanae Takata grew up all over the world and found art to be a universal language. She studied at Parsons the New School for Design to further explore the power of creativity. Nanae now works as a fashion designer for a renowned Japanese company in New York City.

Tracy Turnbull studied Fashion at Newcastle Polytechnic, graduating in 1992 with a BA hons. She has more than 13 years' experience working as a garment designer and illustrator. She currently teaches at Northumbria University's School of Art and Design, teaching across both the Fashion Marketing and Fashion Design courses. She specializes in digital fashion illustration and presentation skills, helping students create and prepare innovative professional portfolios.

All step-by-step and other images are the copyright of Quarto Publishing plc. While every effort has been made to credit contributors, Quarto would like to apologize should there have been any omissions or errors—and would be pleased to make the appropriate correction for future editions of the book.

Author's acknowledgments

I would like to thank my mother, Delbar Jenab, my father, Ray Tahmasebi, and my brother, Shayan Tahmasebi.

Thank you to: Lindsay Kaubi, Jackie Palmer, Kate Kirby, Sorrel Wood, Susi Martin, and the team at Quarto.

I would also like to thank my teachers: Carol Bishop, Mark Westermore, Nancy Riegelman, Rod Langman, Vanessa Newsome.

Many thanks to: Lorrie Ivas, chair of the fashion department at AIU, American Intercontinental University, Fashion Institute of Design and Merchandising, and my students.

Thanks to the following models, who posed for the majority of the figures in this book: Diami Sotomayor, Dahye Lee, Alicia Sixtos, Ashley Semerc, Stacy Syroka, Donna Letterese, Fernando Landeros.

Thanks to the models and designers Dahye Katie Lee and Ashley Semerc for contributing some of their own clothing designs. Garments 60, 73, and 78 are designed by Dahye Lee. Garments 64 and 72 are designed by Ashley Semerc.

Some garments are based on designs by: Banana Republic, BCBG, Bebe, Guess?, H&M, J. Crew, Nathalia Gaviria, and Trina Turk.